LIVE SIMPLY

So That Others Might Simply Live

Peter van Kampen

Perpetua Press
Box 468
Caroline, Alberta
T0M 0M0
www.perpetuapress.ca

Library and Archives Canada Cataloguing in Publication

Title: Live Simply So Others Might Simply Live

Names: van Kampen, Peter

Description: Nonfiction

ISBN: 978-1-0690414-2-5

Second Edition with discussion questions

Cover and book design by Perpetua Press

DEDICATION

To my wife,

Thanks for being my inspiration.

Riches are not forbidden, but the pride of them is.

~ John Chrysostom ~

CONTENTS

Introduction

This book is intended for a very specific audience. It is intended for people who both give their assent of faith to the Church—meaning that they choose to believe what the Church teaches—and who also take seriously the universal call to holiness.

I say this right off the bat because the message that I am going to share is a difficult and challenging one. I built this challenging message on the infallible teachings of the Church and on the standard of holiness, so people who do not agree with these precepts will invariably disagree with my conclusions.

The message is this: we are all called to "live simply, so that others might simply live" (in the words variously attributed to Mother Teresa, St. Elizabeth Ann Seton and Mahatma Gandhi). I believe that this is God's radical call for every Christian who is seeking to do His will and to be sanctified by His Spirit. But a life of simplicity is profoundly countercultural in western countries, even in Christian circles. Moreover, with the exception of Pope Francis, this teaching does not seem to be frequently articulated by the leaders in our churches.

I believe that this is the call of God, particularly in, and for, our times. In some ways the message is analogous to the Church's teaching on contraception: like the Church's teaching on contraception, her teaching on money is profoundly countercultural, requires a lot of personal sacrifice, and will accordingly be rejected by people unless they both actively choose to believe what the Church teaches over their own inclinations and are willing to make the sacrifices necessary to grow in holiness.

We are all called to live simply so that we can give more to the poor. By living simply, I am suggesting something more than the standard call to "generosity" and even more than tithing, which the more radical among us do. I believe that as Christians we ought to live in a way that is noticeably different from our contemporaries with regards to money. We should be accumulating fewer goods, living in smaller houses, and going on fewer vacations. The money that we save can be given to help the poor. I want to suggest that so far, we are not doing that. Our houses are just as ornate, our cars just as powerful, our clothing just as nice, and our vacations just as elaborate as anyone else's.

Just as different communities in the Church have different charisms—some are Marian, others evangelists, others teachers, others contemplative, etc.—I considered making the case that some, but not all, are called to simplicity, and writing a book that would be convicting for a few while letting the others off the hook. Maybe the call to simplicity is just for a select few who feel the prompting in their hearts to follow this particular charism.

But honestly, I don't think anyone is exempt from this call, any more than any faithful Catholic is exempt from the call to reject contraception. Just as some are called to celibacy, but all are called to chastity, so some are called to poverty, but all are called to simplicity!

But don't take my word for it. I intend to demonstrate that this teaching, challenging as it is, has been the teaching of the Catholic Church for two thousand years, continues to be the clearly articulated teaching of the Church today, is emphasized by Pope Francis as head of the Church, and is clearly taught in the Bible both by Christ and His Apostles.

I believe that the call to simplicity can be transformative both for us as individuals as well as for the world in which we live. It is a hard teaching, but like every teaching of the Church, it leads to a deeper satisfaction and joy than we could have otherwise known.

Live Simply So Others Might Simply Live

Chapter One

Learning To Live Simply

Live simply so that others might simply live. More than just a nice idea or clever bumper sticker, this is a moral imperative for all Christians. It is scriptural, it is the teaching of the Catholic Church, and frankly it is the reasonable application of the virtue of compassion and of the principle of "loving your neighbour as yourself." It seems self-evident to me that we are not loving our neighbours as ourselves or doing unto others as we would have them do unto us if we let them starve while we live in luxury. But despite all of this, living simply is an imperative largely ignored by wealthy, western Christians.

My journey with simplicity began about fifteen years ago now, when I was living in Ottawa. At that time, I was living in a household with five other young Catholic men. The house was a small townhouse, so it could be argued that the six of us were already living simply, but this was due to necessity, not choice.

In those days, I had a very active social life; in fact, we had a small community of young adults directly involved in the youth ministry that I was coordinating. Several of them would spend their days with me in the office, would attend daily Mass with me, and then go to prayers in the evening at the Grotto.

When we weren't praying, we were playing Ultimate Frisbee or Mario Kart or going to Perkins for food, or frankly, doing whatever we wanted. But I kept struggling with this nagging sensation, especially when whatever we were doing cost money.

I was tithing faithfully, and some of my money was going towards my two sponsor children through Compassion Canada. Winrose Kagendo was from Kenya, and Ishimwe Claudette was from Rwanda. At that time, most sponsor organizations—Compassion, World Vision, and my personal favourite, Chalice— charged about thirty dollars per month to sponsor a child.

Thirty dollars was a convenient amount because it translated to roughly one dollar per day. If I spent fourteen dollars to watch a movie with my friends, I found that my conscience would be nagging at me the whole time I was watching it because I could have fed, clothed and educated a child in Africa for fourteen days. Instead, I selfishly consumed a movie. Movies were the worst; at least when I was eating at Perkins, I would usually be finished eating before the guilt set in.

Maybe I have a natural advantage in the challenge of living simply compared to other people. I have a heart for it. And people who know me will tell you that I have very little desire to dress fashionably in the latest clothes, or drive hot cars, or have the hippest furniture. I can happily do without the luxuries a lot of our culture enjoys.

And yet I wasn't doing without. At least, as I said, not by choice. If I had money, I would first tithe and then spend my money selfishly on whatever satisfied my whims. I would have these regular and growing inclinations to do something about my guilty conscience, but they resulted in very little action. I would even go to confession and confess "spending my time and money selfishly instead of generously," make my act of contrition in which I firmly resolved to be different...and then I would proceed to act no differently.

I remember one day when my glasses were in ill repair (I was trying to bring back the masking tape look), and a friend told me I should buy new ones. I had no benefits through my employer at that time.

"Well," I told her, "I could spend two hundred dollars on a new pair of glasses, or I could give the money to the poor."

"Are you going to give it to the poor?" she challenged me.

"No," I admitted. And I didn't. Neither did I buy glasses at that time. Instead, I just whittled my money away on frivolities.

Still, my conviction grew. I am not sure why. I suspect that it had something to do with my prayer habits at that time. St. Maximilian Kolbe taught that the formula for holiness is w=W, where the lowercase 'w' represents our will and the uppercase 'W' is God's will. Our will must be identical to God's will. As someone who was a youth minister who had spent a year at the John Paul II

Catholic Bible School and two years in the seminary, the idea that "we are all called to be saints" was something I firmly believed and taught. So, in my prayer time, I would regularly renew my intention to become a saint, by God's grace. This would mean conforming my will to the will of God.

I was in the habit of praying the Stations of the Cross most evenings at the Grotto of our Lady of Lourdes. The Grotto is a quiet, prayerful place, right in Vanier, one of the rougher areas of Ottawa. There is a large stone grotto featuring a statue of the Blessed Virgin and commemorating her apparition to St. Bernadette of Lourdes. Along the outside of the garden are large, illuminated Stations of the Cross. I went there almost every night to pray, sometimes with friends.

I developed my own way of praying the Stations of the Cross, wherein for each station, instead of reading someone else's reflections, I would meditate on the station for a moment and then pray something that I thought tied in. For instance, at the first station where "Jesus is condemned to death," I prayed for our politicians—that they would make sound judgments based in truth—and that I would not be judgmental and not place too much stake in what others thought of me.

For the tenth station, I always considered how Jesus was stripped of His garments and how He allowed people to take everything He had away from Him. So, I would pray for the same sense of detachment—that if there were anything that was coming between me and God, that He would either allow that thing to be taken away from me or give me the grace to give it up of my own accord. This, I knew, was a very dangerous prayer. Once as a young man in Calgary, I had prayed it in the middle of the night while in adoration. I then walked out to discover that my bike had been stolen!

I believe now that this prayer for detachment changed me. Søren Kierkegaard famously said, "Prayer does not change God, but it changes him who prays." If holiness is w=W, then it stands to reason that the best thing to do to mold your will to God's is to spend time in prayer. In prayer you continually resolve to want the things that God wants—at least if your prayer life has evolved past the most elementary levels. It feels ridiculous to turn to God in prayer and ask for selfish things, like wealth or personal glory or revenge. To choose to pray about the things foremost in your mind is to choose to let God change the way you think about them.

I believe that because I took this issue to prayer, God changed my heart with regards to materialism. But even grace and guilt did not seem to be enough to make a real change in me. For this God needed to use Catherine, the woman I would later marry.

I moved back to Calgary and began a dating relationship with Catherine at around the same time. Catherine and I had known each other for nine years, since we attended Bible school together, and had both lived in Ottawa for several years and had the same circle of friends. When we started dating, we discussed this notion I had that I was spending my money selfishly and should do otherwise. Catherine did not share my appreciation for movies and deep-fried Perkins fare and was more disciplined overall in the way she spent her money. She challenged me to move my conviction from a vague idea and start taking some concrete steps. It was only once I did this that I really began to understand the idea of simplicity.

When I was in the seminary, I lived with a priest (now bishop) named Fr. Scott McCaig. He often repeated the maxim that "exterior discipline leads to interior conversion." I know that I ought to be praying more, but unless I made a plan and start getting up in the morning, I probably never would. The same goes for eating healthier or getting more exercise or resisting temptation…we need not just good intentions but also a concrete exterior discipline that, once put into practice, will eventually become internalized and change our hearts.

So challenged by Catherine, I implemented an exterior discipline. And it has been a game changer, although I didn't even realize it at the time. I started what I call my "luxury budget." This is an extremely simple concept: I limit my expenses to only one hundred dollars a month on things that I do not need. Because I limit my consumption of luxuries, this frees up a lot of money to give away. Soon after I implemented this discipline on myself, Catherine started it as well. Ten years later, we still maintain the luxury budget.

But here's the thing: my whole argument for simplicity is that in light of the fact that people in the world are starving and suffering in innumerable other ways due to their poverty, we as Christians who "love our neighbours as ourselves" should be prepared to make sacrifices for them to help them. And yet, even when I restrict myself, I still allow myself one hundred dollars a month on things that I clearly do not need but that I only want. So, before anybody goes off and starts the canonization process for me or my wife, please note that this is actually an extremely selfish thing that we are doing. But it is at least a start.

The brilliant thing about the luxury budget, and the reason it is the number one way in which I recommend people begin practicing the virtue of simplicity, is that it quickly leads to more than you initially realize. When I made the commitment, most of my luxury budget was consumed by eating out unnecessarily, entertainment, and other luxuries such as alcohol and Coca-Cola and Tim Hortons coffee. Indeed, I had no idea that I was spending so much on unnecessary consumables. Before I started the budget, these things were basically unchecked and were considered part of the cost of living. Once I set a limit and started keeping track of my expenses, I was at least prevented from buying these things without consideration.

In truth, this was all the budget was intended to do. I would not consume a Coke, so I could give another dollar and a half to the poor as a result.

Another cool thing I started doing was buying gifts for my wife out of my luxury budget. The reason this is cool is because now that we're married, we have a joint account. Theoretically without the luxury budget, I could buy her a seven-hundred-dollar gift and wow her at Christmas, but the truth is that she may not actually appreciate me spending seven hundred dollars of our money on that particular gift. Instead, I might get her a seventy-dollar gift, and she knows that in order to do so, I actually made a significant sacrifice from my own personal budget. I believe that doing so makes the gifts we give to each other more meaningful, while at the same time keeping them simple.

But here is what I didn't see coming: suppose I am in a store, and I see a new shirt that I would like to own. Do I need it? If not, or if I could reasonably expect to fill that need more affordably at a secondhand store, then the purchase is a luxury. Even then if you have low standards and little fashion sense, as I do, you can get away with ten-dollar shirts at Walmart. But what about when you want new shoes? Or technology? Or a second car? Or furniture for your house? Or unnecessary renovations to your house? Or a fancy vacation?

You see the problem? I started a luxury budget with the idea that it would limit my social life and my consumption of things such as alcohol, but instead it has had massive implications on my entire lifestyle. Every time I make a purchase, I need to make the decision: is this a necessity, or is it a luxury?

That is how the exterior discipline eventually led to my interior conversion. Because now I am convicted that I should not be enjoying all the luxuries that my contemporaries enjoy, even though I can afford them, even after tithing.

Okay, so I must admit that I am not entirely legalistic about the budget. If you were to implement one yourself, you would obviously need to use your judgment and an informed conscience. For example, depending on your line of work, it may be important that you wear a certain quality of clothing, and so you may have to spend money accordingly.

Some people get confused when I talk about this and think that I am suggesting we should not get high-paying jobs or seek advancement in our careers. By no means! After all, the more money you make, the more you can give away. If you have weighed it in your conscience, and you think it is important that you wear expensive clothes in order to do your job effectively, then do so. But don't do it without first both informing and examining your conscience.

My wife and I have decided to consider certain things "necessities," although clearly, they really are not: we allow ourselves one date a month, complete with the cost of dinner and babysitting. We give gifts to our kids at Christmas and birthdays without counting that as a luxury. On days when we go to the hospital (which are all too frequent in my household), we will allow ourselves to buy a nice meal at a restaurant—well, a meal at a fast-food joint, but still. If we take the kids to the beach, we don't deduct the unnecessary gas expense from our luxury budget. We do go camping in the summer. You get the idea.

For Catherine and me, we began this budget at an interesting point in our lives. We were not yet married, and we had not yet acquired many goods. We kept our wedding itself fairly simple: the meal was potluck and Catherine's dress was her white graduation dress that her mom repurposed by sewing beautiful gold sheer fabric onto it. But then we allowed ourselves an expensive honeymoon in Sedona, Arizona. I suspect that, after ten years of living simply, we would not allow ourselves so nice a honeymoon now.

Even the wedding rings had to go under the scrutiny of our value system. For example, for our engagement ring, Catherine wanted an aquamarine rather than a diamond. This is because she knew that the diamond engagement ring was the result of a cleverly devised marketing campaign by De Beers, which at one point controlled 90% of the world's diamond production. So effective was the campaign and product placement in Hollywood that today the idea of a diamond engagement ring is ubiquitous in North American society, with standard etiquette being that it should be valued at two months' salary.

Rebelling against that cultural norm, I set out to find the ring that Catherine requested, a simple gold band with a princess-cut aquamarine in it. Not able to find it, I asked the jeweler.

"For a promise ring, right?" she prompted.

"No, an engagement ring."

At this she exhaled audibly, and the expression on her face clearly indicated that she thought I was pathetic and that my proposal was doomed to be rejected (unless of course the woman I was asking was even more pathetic than me). Needless to say, I bought my ring elsewhere.

Her response surprised me. Our culture has embraced these materialistic values so completely that the idea of someone rebelling against them is preposterous. And the truth is, I did give Catherine an engagement ring made of gold with a gemstone in it, albeit not a diamond. I did succumb that far to the expectations of luxury that our culture has for us. We also bought gold wedding bands for each of us.

I remember feeling conflicted about my wedding band: the significance in it lay in the sacrament Catherine and I shared, but I wondered if I needed something so expensive to give due honour to that sacrament. I felt like Oskar Schindler, the famous Nazi industrialist who saved the lives of some 1,200 Jews during World War II by employing them.

At the end of the movie Schindler's List (1993), instead of celebrating the heroic way in which he saved so many lives, Schindler is tormented by the fact that he could have saved more with the gold and luxuries he had retained for himself. He looks at his pin and says "This pin. Two people. This is gold. Two more people. He would have given me two for it, at least one. One more person."

So, I would look at my three-hundred-dollar wedding ring and question its value. Remember that three hundred dollars translated into three hundred days of necessities for a child somewhere. It's tough to claim that I "love my neighbour as myself" when I allow myself such luxury at their expense.

After the wedding, I considered selling the ring, but of course you never get much return on such items. In the end the decision was taken from me when I lost the ring while playing Capture the Flag in the forest at the Catholic summer camp I worked for. It is important that I still wear a wedding ring, since such a great number of young ladies find me incredibly attractive and it is better to disappoint them early, but today my wedding ring is a one-dollar souvenir from a convent in Kenya.

That Kenya trip was the next major development in my theories about simplicity. I travelled with Renewal Ministries and served as a teacher in parishes and for catechists. Until I went to Kenya, I never really knew what poverty was. I had been to Mexico and had done service putting roofs on houses in remote mountain regions. There I developed a greater love for the poor, an appreciation for the luxury and comfort we live in, and, in particular a zeal to never waste food. In the words of Pope Francis, "Throwing food away is like stealing it from the poor and hungry."[1] In Kenya my eyes were opened even more, and throughout this book I will include stories from the trips I've made to Kenya, Tanzania, and Mexico that illustrate my point.

---

[1] Francis I, Twitter post (June 7, 2013), retrieved from https://twitter.com/pontifex/status/342930680570855425?lang=en.

By the time I visited Kenya, I had already been living with my luxury budget for three years, so I was accustomed to living self-sacrificially and giving my money to the poor. The trip by the way was free and paid for by the generosity of others. But we had long stopovers in London and Dubai, where my travel companion, Chris, and I were able to see the sights and where I allowed myself some license with my money.

In Kenya we had resolved that we would have time for a quick, four-hour safari at the end of the trip. We would go to Nairobi National Park, a small park right beside city limits where one could expect to see giraffes, zebras, hippos, baboons, crocodiles, and lions (although not elephants). As a wildlife enthusiast—as in the kind of guy who makes as little noise as possible when walking in the Canadian Rockies in hopes of seeing a large predator—this was a very exciting idea for me!

And yet I was conflicted. Every day I was telling people in Kenya about the love of God, and building relationships with them, and seeing how they lived. And the inconsistency between their lives and my own shocked me.

I knew about poverty—by then my wife and I had accumulated a number of sponsor children and had been noting their cute pictures of their homes and their cooking huts and knew that some of their families were not even able to provide the most basic goods—but I suppose I didn't really understand the full extent of it.

My first week in Kenya we stayed in a compound in Embulbul, near the Ngong Hills Nature Reserve. We stayed in the compound the first few days because we were afraid to walk in the streets. I don't know yet how legitimate my fear was; some people seemed to think it was silly, and others that it was very wise. The trouble was that everywhere we went, people would see the msungus, a word meaning "foreigners" or "white people," roaming the streets, and everyone would know that we were "rich." And frankly, rich foreigners make easy targets.

Normally I don't think of myself as rich. I'm a Catholic youth minister—which means I'm not exactly in the highest grossing salary bracket in Canada. But once I wandered outside the compound, the degree of wealth I enjoyed was impressed upon me.

I was a tourist, and I wanted to take photos of everything. At that time the only camera I had was one of the ones with the great big lenses that you have to hang around your neck. And for most of the people I saw in that area, my camera was worth more than everything they owned put together! I became too ashamed to carry it with me and flaunt my wealth. Many of these people lived in a small shack made of mud and corrugated tin for a home, which would probably be condemned if constructed as even a shed in Canada. For a wardrobe, they might have had a small pile of secondhand clothes, much of which Value Village would throw out if anyone had been rude enough to donate it to them.

I came to know one young man, Steve, who brought me to his home. He shared a single room with three adult brothers. When I asked where they went to the bathroom, he indicated the field behind his house where people dumped their garbage. Then he explained to me that women felt particularly threatened if they went during the day, so they would try to hold it until night and go in the dark. Of course, if a man did want to take advantage of a woman, he knew where to wait. I will return to Steve's story later.

As the weeks went on, my eyes continued to be opened. By the kids playing football (soccer) with a tied-up clump of garbage and no shoes. By the girl whose filthy dress had become torn from her chest down and then tied closed with a rag. Or by the priest who answered me when we drove past withered corn fields in the rural areas, and I ignorantly asked about irrigation.

"Irrigation?" the priest driving me said. "They don't even have drinking water!"

He went on to tell me about how people in that region would have to go to the river for their water. It was filthy dirty, and they gathered it in dirty water containers and brought it home to their families. Moreover, while getting water, people were frequently taken by crocodiles.

By the time we arrived at our third location, it was really starting to grate on me. We were staying in the coastal city of Malindi, and each day we would drive out to Marafa, about an hour's drive into rural territory, to teach our classes. Malindi has a tourist economy, and other msungus, especially Italians, could be found there. I found myself resenting the other msungus as they seemed to treat all the locals like servants. I hated that the local people I met saw me as one of them. I remember one beautiful local girl, Flavia, being so excited that Chris and I were speaking with her because, as she put it, she had never spoken to whites before.

"What do you mean?" I asked, "You work in a hotel full of Italians!"

"They don't really speak to us," she said, and I was left with the distinct impression that racism was at work there.

The reason that we stayed in Malindi was because there was nowhere suitable for msungus to stay in Marafa— that is, no hotels with flush toilets and mosquito nets and the quality of food that we were accustomed to. The fact that we were unwilling to lower our standards bothered me, but to be honest, I don't know that I would arrange it any differently.

So, we would drive the hour out past some of the most desperate poverty I'd seen yet. All along the way, there would be children sitting by the side of the road, just waiting for msungus to drive by. When they saw us, they would presume we were Italian and would run after our vehicles yelling, "Ciao! Ciao!" The more clever ones would yell, "Ciao Bella!"

On the way back to Malindi, they would run after us with even more enthusiasm. I was unable to determine the reason why. Until the last day.

That day, a group of Italian tourists came to Marafa. They stopped where we were teaching outdoors, so I welcomed them to join us at the mission. I distinctly remember one attractive blond, woman in her twenties coming and sitting on a chair, and a small local child coming and sitting in her lap, and her openly weeping. It turned out that the reason why she and other tourists came to Marafa was because there is a landform near there called Hell's Kitchen within reddish hoodoos similar to the Grand Canyon.

When we went to Hell's Kitchen, we discovered a salesman selling packages of candy or pencils and notebooks. This explained the phenomenon of the children running after us yelling "Ciao!" Tourists who came there and saw the villages were so moved by the poverty that they felt compelled to do something for the children they saw, however small.

By that time, I was feeling totally conflicted. I still wanted to go on the safari, but how could I justify spending a hundred dollars on four hours of entertainment when the locals were going without?

Every evening, we would find a restaurant in Malindi where we could eat, and usually the fare was pretty good. I felt that I should at least eat more simply so that I could give more money to someone. I didn't have any Kenya shillings of my own; when I arrived there, I was under the impression that I would just find a bank machine and use my debit card to get shillings from my account. Turns out they don't have bank machines in Marafa! This probably dramatically reduced my spending on gifts for people I met.

I asked our team leader for enough shillings so that I could buy a cheap meal, and then I went on my own to the ocean to pray and to think. I waded out into the Indian Ocean, and I began to pray a prayer that is probably the most earnest prayer I have ever prayed.

My prayer was a plea with God. How could I ever justify spending money selfishly on luxuries when people in the world were literally dying from hunger or from a lack of water or basic hygiene? How could I call myself a Christian, whom people would "know by their love," if I did not love my neighbour as myself so much as to give up a little piece of entertainment when it could mean that neighbour's survival? I was yelling and crying into the crash of the ocean, and Bible verses and quotes from the saints kept coming to me, such as "live simply so that others might simply live" and "blessed are the poor" and "woe to you rich" and "the love of money is the root of all evil" and "it's harder for a rich man to enter Heaven than for a camel to pass through the eye of a needle" and "give until it hurts" and "if you have two coats, give to the man who has none," and on and on and on. I felt as though these verses and quotes were crashing on me like the waves of the sea! And I wondered: when is it enough? At what point am I sacrificing enough?

After this experience, I went to a small restaurant and ordered a falafel; when I came outside, I realized that while I was inside, the sun had set. Malindi has very few street lights, so I then had to choose between two frightening prospects: return to the hotel the way I had come, along a lonely and desolate stretch of beach where no one would see me if anything were to happen, or wander through the city, which I did not know well, starting in the Muslim district in a city known for action by groups like Al Shabaab. (Incidentally, the hotel I stayed at in Mpeketoni has since been attacked and burned down by Al Shabaab. Renewal Ministries no longer travels to those regions.)

I opted to wander through the city, and besides one close encounter with a pickpocket and another with two prostitutes soliciting me, as well as the disheartening experience of wandering lost for half an hour only to find myself once again back at the falafel place, I eventually did make it back without incident.

In the end, I did go on the safari. I decided that the discipline of the luxury budget was suitable, and while it is my goal to become a saint, I wanted to maintain a discipline that I felt was realistic. I sometimes liken the journey towards sainthood to lifting weights. Too large a weight will hurt you and not make you stronger. But too light a weight will not challenge you enough to allow you to grow. It should be expected that as you grow, you will be able to take on bigger weights. I find I'm usually inclined to lift a little weight so that I can say, "Yes, I do lift, bro" but not enough that it will challenge me or cause me to grow. In the case of giving to the poor, I felt that at that time a hundred dollars was an appropriate luxury budget, and I did not want to move to too extreme a discipline.

I came home from my Kenya experience deeply and emotionally convicted. The emotional aspect of it caught me off-guard. I have never been one to cry much (if ever) in my adult life. But one day I was giving a talk about my experience in Kenya at a prayer group, and part way through, when I was explaining that the poor are suffering more than we know, I suddenly lost control and started crying publicly. Apparently, my face was so distorted, and my voice gone so suddenly that those who saw me thought I was about to become violently ill. It was completely unexpected, and I was embarrassed.

Today, nine years and several trips later, I still become emotional whenever I speak publicly about it. I'm really hoping it'll wear off eventually, although I've been told that it shows my heart is authentically behind the message and perhaps makes the message more powerful.

I do public speaking on a regular basis, but interestingly it is this message that I receive the most commendation for and am asked most frequently to speak again on. I find it fascinating because it is such a countercultural message, and one that so few voices in the Catholic world are speaking about. I am increasingly convinced that this is the message of the Holy Spirit to the Church today, and that more and more voices will join mine and that of Pope Francis in the coming years.

I am astounded by the frequency with which this message is supported both in scripture and in Church teaching. Pope Francis and the Catechism of the Catholic Church have been bolder on this issue than I would ever dare to be.

For my own part, I continue to keep the luxury budget, and in truth, I love it! I honestly think my life is much richer and more fulfilling because of it. Catherine and I have both since reduced our budgets, and a couple of years ago, we took another dramatic step: we downsized from a nice two-story, three-bedroom home in town to a thousand-square-foot mobile home on rented land in the country.

Our thinking was that we could pay slightly less than we already were, have the place paid off in five years, and then be mortgage-free. In fact, we paid it off even more quickly than that, and I am so excited about how much more money that has freed up for us to give now!

But even downsizing our home, which I thought would be a major and dramatic sacrifice, has proven to be a huge blessing for our family. The only thing that hurts about it is my pride: the stigma attached to mobile homes, and the fact that parts of the exterior are old and shabby looking. Since it's still functional, I decided that a facelift would be a luxury, not a necessity. But it is easily enough space for my family, and I honestly have never loved a house as much as this little one.

To recap: I was convicted first by prayer that simplicity was right. I was converted by the exterior discipline of the luxury budget so that I just keep wanting to live more and more simply. I was confirmed in my theories through my readings of scripture and the teachings of the Church. The whole process is an ongoing work of grace in our lives and has brought a surprising amount of peace and joy!

Chapter One Discussion Questions

1. Peter asserts that "Living Simply" is a Christian principle that is largely ignored by wealthy, western Christians. Do you agree? Why do you think Christians don't talk about this more?

2. "Prayer doesn't change God, but it changes him who prays." Soren Kierkegaard. Do you pray that your spending habits will be conformed to the will of God? When the opportunity to give or to spend arises, do you typically submit the idea to God and try to do His will, or do you just make your own decisions?

3. Exterior discipline leads to interior conversion. Peter recommended the discipline of the luxury budget. Have you applied that? Or have you thought of another, concrete thing you could do to live more simply and generously? Have you noticed an interior conversion?

4. There are societal pressures to live in luxury, like having a diamond engagement ring. Do you feel pressured to keep up with the latest fashions or tech or to vacation like your peers?

5. Peter talked about how seeing poor people in Africa and Mexico impacted his perceptions of wealth and disparity. Have you ever witnessed for yourself how the poor live? Did this impact you?

6. Peter talked about how the decision to live simply, which he thought would be difficult, has been a blessing. Has that been your experience?

Chapter Two
Common Objections

I feel like living simply is one of those things that every Christian knows we should be doing, but most of us aren't bothering to do it. Maybe it goes with other things such as "Pray daily" and "Put others first" and "Jesus came to serve, not to be served, and we should do likewise." We all know these are Christian precepts, and yet most of us will readily admit that we are not serving or praying as much as we should.

Typically, everyone acknowledges that making sacrifices to give to the poor is a good and admirable thing. In fact, when I've raised this topic, almost everyone has affirmed my conclusions, and those that haven't did not challenge me on the principle, but rather on the degree. This is fair. We don't want to be like the Pharisees, who Jesus said would "lay heavy burdens on people" and make it difficult for people to follow God (cf. Matthew 23:4).

Perhaps we are all called to live simply…but we don't all have to have only two outfits, and a wash pan like Mother Teresa. Nor are we all called to move to mobile homes and drive fifteen-year-old minivans. This is, of course, true. But I think most of us in the West are called to a higher degree of simplicity than what we are currently living.

Maybe the reason that so few people speak on this is that neither the Church nor scripture prescribes the degree to which we ought to give. I think this is for good reason.

We like legalism. We like really precise guidelines. You can see this in the manner in which we obey laws, the manner in which we govern our countries, and in the manner in which we discuss ethics. The Catholic Church said unequivocally that we are not to use artificial contraception, and so every obedient Catholic at least knows whether or not their lives are in line with Church teaching in this regard. But the Church has not and cannot say, "This is precisely the line at which you must no longer accumulate wealth."

Even old guidelines like the tithe, giving 10% of our income away, have gone by the wayside, and perhaps this is in part because it was being abused; rich people were only giving 10%, giving out of their excess, while the poor gave 10% and were unable to make ends meet.

Living simply is a matter of conscience, and so it is not for me or even Pope Francis to specify the degree to which we ought to do it. This is part of the transformative nature of the Gospel, where the "law is written on our hearts" (cf. Jeremiah 31:33). Let us not allow the fact that the virtue of simplicity cannot be easily reduced to a dogmatic legalism prevent us from exploring it and attempting to grow in it.

But I do want to answer the objections, however few, that I have received.

Objection:

Not everyone in scripture lived simply.

Take Solomon, for example…

Response: Okay, so that may not be the strongest form of that argument. Clearly Solomon with his seven hundred wives and three hundred concubines may not have been living precisely the ethical life that we are called to live. But in the Old Testament in particular, there are others who live in wealth. Consider Abraham, David, or Esther. For each of these you may be able to say that they were rich but did not hold undue affection for their wealth. Isn't that what we as Christians are called to do?

I believe that Christ in fact called us to more than that. Nearly every author in the New Testament warns us about the dangers of wealth and the importance of love for the poor. It may be that living in wealth and tithing in the Old Testament was acceptable under the Old Covenant, with its legalisms and promise of land and prosperity as rewards for the covenant, while in the New Testament we are called to more.

However, even in the Old Testament, a careful examination of the scriptures will reveal that when the covenant was broken, it was not merely as a result of the people worshipping idols but often because the prophets were warning them against living in wealth while failing to provide for widows and orphans. We will return to these arguments later.

Objection:

"But didn't Jesus once say,

'The poor will always be with you?'"

Response: Um…yup. This is one of the few New Testament passages that seems to imply that we ought not concern ourselves with the poor; however, if you take it on balance with the rest of the New Testament, it becomes evident that that is not what Christ was trying to say. I suppose it indicates that the goal of eradicating poverty is not a realistic one, but the idea that we should alleviate the suffering of the poor remains a very strong scriptural principle.

Objection:

The Church exists to evangelize, and so we must live like wealthy people in order to be credible with wealthy people.

Response: Perhaps—but let's imagine that after tithing a family is living on $100,000 per year. Suppose that, living simply, they could make do on $70,000 per year. Is it conceivable that there is a more effective way to spend $30,000 to evangelize than by maintaining your beautiful home? Suppose a church gave you $30,000 with a mandate to evangelize, and you spent that money on improvements to your home where you maybe hosted Bible studies and out-of-town guests on occasion—would that be good stewardship of your funds? Could you justify it? Or is this an example of what St. Basil of Caesarea was talking about when he said, "by a certain wily artifice of the devil, countless pretexts of expenditure are proposed to the rich"?[2]

Objection:

"We enjoy a wealthy lifestyle

for the sake of our children, our primary vocation."

Response: This objection has the obvious flaw that it presumes that providing a wealthy lifestyle is good for the children, while I'm arguing that it is quite possibly damaging to their souls. I will demonstrate that both scripture and Church teaching consider the love of wealth to be a source of woe and the root of all evil, which chokes the Word and makes it almost impossible to enter the kingdom.

Obviously, the wealthy lifestyle can and probably does include things such as formative experiences, sports and art classes, and faith-based movies and reading material. As I said before, the matter of degree is not defined by the Church or scripture, and it is not my intention to define it. This means that it is a matter of conscience for parents when they consider what programs to enroll their children in and how much to provide. What about costly Catholic schools? Can I put my daughter in ballet while my sponsor child desperately needs AIDS medication?

To the person who maintains that their wealthy lifestyle is for the sake of their children, I ask: Is it your

[2] St. Basil the Great, "Sermon to the Rich," s.2, retrieved from http://stjohngoc.org/st-basil-the-greats-sermon-to-the-rich/.

intention to begin living simply once they move out?

Objection:

"Jesus said to love your neighbour,

not people on the other side of the planet."

Response: There may be valid arguments to be made about having a higher concern for people in our own countries as opposed to people somewhere else. But I do not believe that the man who said, "love your enemies" and used the parable of the Good Samaritan to illustrate what He meant by the word "neighbour" would have us differentiate among people based only on proximity, especially in an age when we can so easily help people overseas.

Often when I get into a conversation about ideas such as helping refugees or sponsoring people in other countries, people say, "Why don't we help the people in our country first?" I admit that I don't really get that argument, because I don't think the two ideas are mutually exclusive and I suspect that those who develop a spirit of compassion for the poor are likely to help in both places. Perhaps our government has greater responsibility for people in our own country, but as individuals responding in compassion, I think the precept that in the Church "there is neither Jew nor Greek"[3] may apply here. Some Christians have responded by dividing their alms: two-thirds to local initiatives and one-third to foreign initiatives. For my

---

[3] Galatians 3:28

part, I prefer to give overseas as I get so much more "bang for my buck"—that is, I can improve individuals' lives so much more for the same amount of money. But that is a matter of preference and discernment.

Objection:

If it is true that all Catholics are called to simplicity, wouldn't you expect other Catholic leaders to write and speak about this topic?

Response: I must admit, I think this is the single best argument against my whole philosophy. I am trying to make the case that it is self-evident that you cannot "love your neighbour as yourself" if you live in luxury while your neighbour goes without basic necessities. Further, I hope to demonstrate that this idea is clearly scriptural, the explicit teaching of the Catholic Church, and the consistent teaching of saints throughout the centuries. Surely if I am right about all of this, others would be teaching it.

Frankly, if they were teaching it, I wouldn't feel the need to write this book myself. If you think I'm overstating this, conduct an experiment. Go to the library at your parish or check out the CD collection from Lighthouse Catholic Media and see how many authors are addressing the ethical use of money.

So why aren't they? I don't know; I can only speculate. There are cynical possibilities. Perhaps it is because the message of simplicity is so unpopular that those who teach it are not published or do not become famous speakers. Maybe Catholic publishers are afraid of this challenging message. Maybe it is because this happens to be the error of our time, and just as Catholic leaders in former times would have had the biases of their times in their writings—be it Jansenism or antisemitism or a belief in fairies—so perhaps leaders today do not even recognize that they are wrong about this.

I suspect, however, that it is merely a difference in emphasis. Catholic authors and speakers might say that the purpose of life is to bring glory to God, and since the glory of God is man fully alive (according to St. Irenaeus), then our mission in life must be to become the best versions of ourselves. Yes or yes?

This is of course true as far as it goes. But I am arguing that the purpose of life is to love. These two ideas are not antithetical but are complementary. But if you won one million dollars and your mission was to love, you'd likely give it almost all away.

On the other hand, if your mission is to be fully alive—that is, the best version of yourself—you'd likely give some away, but also use a considerable amount on self-improvement, pursuing hobbies, and going on nice vacations. However, I think St. Paul would say something like this: "If I become fully alive and the best version of myself, but I have not love, I am useless."

Add to this the emphasis in some churches of faith over works and the emphasis on a personal relationship with Christ as what definitively makes one a Christian, and the suspicion that many Catholics have of anything that sounds like social justice, and we can conclude that perhaps the teaching on money has simply been overlooked.

There is another even more noble possibility. I am often confronted by the verse that says, "So when you give to the needy, do not announce it with trumpets, as the hypocrites do in the synagogues and on the streets, to be honoured by others. Truly I tell you, they have received their reward in full. But when you give to the needy, do not let your left hand know what your right hand is doing, so that your giving may be in secret. Then your Father, who sees what is done in secret, will reward you." (Matthew 6:2–4)

If I give talks or write books on simplicity, am I just sounding the trumpet, advertising the fact that I give? Perhaps the other Catholic authors and speakers do know the Church teaching and live according to it, but out of humility they don't talk about it. I've often wondered if I should be talking about it, or if I should just give quietly and "not let my left hand know what my right hand is doing." However, if you continue to read that passage, it goes on to talk about the importance of being discreet in our prayer: "But when you pray, go into your room, close the door and pray to your Father, who is unseen. Then your Father, who sees what is done in secret, will reward you." (Matthew 6:6)

When I teach about prayer and I tell people that "these are the prayers I enjoy doing" or "I try to pray so much every day," am I virtue signaling, or am I giving new Christians an example that they can imitate and learn from? Just as I tell people that I do in fact pray and just as I admonish them to pray as well, so I also tell people that I give to the poor and admonish them to do so as well.

I do not know why there are so few books on this topic. But I do hope that through prayerfully reading this book you will be as persuaded as I am that living simply is the correct moral response to our times, and that it is the teaching of Christ, of scripture, and of the Church.

Chapter Two Discussion Questions

1. Have you had people object to your ambitions to live simply? What, in your opinion, is the strongest objection to the idea that we should live simply? How do you answer it?

2. Do you think Christians would be more credible to the wealthy if we lived like them, or if we lived self sacrificially?

3. Peter wrestles with the fact that simplicity seems to be the commonsense response to wealth, espoused by scriptures, saints and Church Fathers, and yet the big name influential catholic speakers and writers don't talk about it. Why do you think this is? Are you aware of any influential Catholics who are addressing this teaching?

4. "So, when you give to the needy, do not announce it with trumpets, as the hypocrites do in the synagogues and on the streets, to be honoured by others. Truly I tell you, they have received their reward in full. But when you give to the needy, do not let your left hand know what your right hand is doing, so that your giving may be in secret. Then your Father, who sees what is done in secret, will reward you." (Matthew 6:2-4) If we are living simply, should we be discreet so as to be humble, or is it justified to talk about it in hopes of inspiring others?

Chapter Three
Teachings of Scripture

There are over two thousand verses in the Bible that address God's concern for the poor. Every author of the New Testament (except Jude) clearly warns us against the love of money, that we cannot serve God and money, that we cannot say we love God if we don't care for the needs of the poor. It is the frequency with which the Bible discusses the correct use of money that stunned me when I became aware of it because it is mentioned so frequently and yet preached on so rarely.

I discovered most of these passages for myself, just from reading the Bible with this thought in mind. At the back of this book, you will find an appendix that lists many of the key scripture passages on money, followed by Church teachings.

However, if you want to see for yourself just how much scripture says about this topic, there may be a more effective way of gaining an appreciation for it. Go to any Bible website with a search engine, such as Bible Gateway (www.biblegateway.com) and run a search on a word like "rich" or "wealth" or "money" or "poor" or "generous" or "greed," and just see what comes up, especially in the New Testament. Scripture addresses the ethical use of money much more frequently than, say, sexual morality. When we distinguish ourselves as Christians from our contemporaries, there should be more than our sexual ethic setting us apart.

And yet regarding money, we are just like our contemporaries. We are supposed to be the "salt of the earth." But if salt loses its saltiness, what good is it? (cf. Matthew 5:13)

Right from the beginning the Gospels challenge us to live differently with regard to money. Before Jesus came, John the Baptist was the voice in the wilderness preparing the way of the Lord and calling people to repentance.

When people begin to realize the urgency of the call to repentance, they ask, "What should we do?"

Look what John says, "Anyone who has two shirts should share with the one who has none, and anyone who has food should do the same." (Luke 3:11)

Then specifically to the tax collectors he says, "Don't collect more than you are required" (Luke 3:13), and to the soldiers, "Do not extort money from anyone." (Luke 3:14)

Isn't that interesting? In all three cases, repentance means changing our attitude regarding money. If John the Baptist told people to repent for having two shirts, what do you think he would say to us if he walked into our homes or looked into our closets? Of course, in John's time, clothing cost much more, and most people had very few garments. It may be appropriate today to have many outfits, but the principle is that if we have more than we need, we ought to share with others rather than accumulate even more.

Jesus Himself said, "If you want to be perfect, go sell your possessions and give to the poor" (Matthew 19:21). Is it safe to assume that He was only speaking to the rich young man when He said this and that we ought not to apply this verse to our own lives?

Really, the whole thing is intuitive. If Jesus commands us to love our neighbour as ourselves, and John tells us that we cannot love God unless we love our neighbour, then it is self-evident that we as Christians must care for the poor. "If anyone has material possessions and sees a brother or sister in need but has no pity on them, how can the love of God be in that person? Dear children, let us not love with words and speech but with actions and in truth." (1 John 3:17–18)

The teaching of the New Testament on this subject might be summarized in this passage from James, "Religion that God our Father accepts as pure and faultless is this: to look after orphans and widows in their distress and to keep oneself from being polluted by the world." (James 1:27)

The Sermon on the Mount

If you want to understand the teachings of Christ on morality, there is no better place to look than in the Sermon on the Mount.

Dr. Timothy Gray called the Sermon on the Mount "the Magna Carta of Social Justice."[4] According to St.

---

[4] Dr. Timothy Gray, *Encountering the Poor: Biblical Roots for Catholic*

Augustine, the Sermon on the Mount provides the "perfect standard for the Christian Life," and if it were all we had—if we had lost the rest of scripture—we would know how to live as Christians.[5] At the heart of the Sermon in Matthew 6, almost the entire chapter has been dedicated to issues relating to money; it discusses giving to the needy (Matthew 6:1–4), storing up treasures in Heaven and not on earth (Matthew 6: 19 21), the impossibility of serving God and money (Matthew 6:24), and not worrying about our physical needs and desires but seeking first the kingdom (Matthew 6: 25–34).

In what is possibly the most important sermon that Christ ever preached, in which is found the perfect standard for Christian life, a major theme is this: as Christians, we cannot serve God and money, so we should not worry about our needs but instead seek the kingdom of God, and give generously to the needy.

Give Until It Hurts

I love the saying attributed to Mother Teresa: "Give until it hurts." Some people will take that even further and say, "Give until it stops hurting," which is a nice idea, but I've never quite gotten that far myself.

Social Teaching [CD], Lighthouse Catholic Media.

[5] St. Augustine, *On the Sermon on the Mount,* Book 1, translated by William Findlay, in *Nicene and Post-Nicene Fathers*, First Series, Vol. 6, edited by Philip Schaff (Buffalo, NY: Christian Literature Publishing Co., 1888), X.

True, there is a freedom in giving, and "God loves a cheerful giver" (2 Corinthians 9–7), but even in that latter passage, the message is to give bountifully and not under compulsion. God is not outdone in generosity, and He transforms our hearts such that we no longer desire the things of this world, so that we are only satisfied with doing His will. This is the nature of grace. Initially, living according to God's design and cooperating with grace may feel like a sacrifice, but in time we are transformed in such a way that our sacrifice becomes a joy.

I think there is a danger when we only give to the degree that we *feel* like giving, responding not to grace but to our natural human desires. The Christian journey is one of constantly giving our will over to the will of God. I think too often Christians have cited 2 Corinthians 9:6–7 as a justification for only giving what they are naturally compelled to give from their own will, rather than giving generously according to the will of God. "Whoever is generous to the poor lends to the Lord, and He will repay him for his deed." (Proverbs 19:17)

There are many passages that deal with the idea that our gift should cost us something and require some self-sacrifice. "I will not sacrifice to the LORD my God burnt offerings that cost me nothing" (2 Samuel 24:24). Often regarding this idea, my wife and I will consider the wealth and ease in which we live, and then ask the question, "Does it hurt yet?" This is not just a catchphrase, but a scriptural principle.

Consider Mark 12:41–44. This is the passage where Jesus sees the widow give her last two coins and praises her by comparing her action to that of the rich people who merely give out of their excess. The tithe can be abused because rich people will suppose that if they give their ten percent, they have done their duty. Obviously even giving ten percent may be more than what many are giving now, and so it is a great starting point. But Jesus was critical of the rich and of the Pharisees, many of whom would have legalistically tithed, but whose gift would still have come out of their excess. Are we like the Pharisees who gave out of our abundance, or are we like the poor widow who was commended for putting in all that she had?

Consider these other passages, with the message repeated again and again that we are to be generous with the poor:

- "Give to everyone who asks you." (Luke 6:30)

- "How joyful are those who fear the Lord…they share freely and give generously to those in need." (Psalm 112:1, 9)

- "Be generous to the poor, and everything will be clean for you." (Luke 11:41)

- "Sell your possessions and give to the poor. Provide purses for yourself that will never wear out, a treasure in Heaven that will never fail, where no thief comes near, and no moth destroys." (Luke 12:33)

- "They gave as much as they were able, and even beyond their ability." (2 Corinthians 8:3)

I want to suggest that while it is obvious that it is a Christian value to be generous with the poor, we are failing to be generous when we only give out of our rather remarkable excess.

Remember what John the Baptist said: "Whoever has two coats must share with anyone who has none. Whoever has food must do likewise." (Luke 3:11)

How many coats do you have?

Not Asceticism

Please note that I am not suggesting that we should all live in poverty or that we should all live ascetic lives. I said earlier that I think that some are called to poverty, but all are called to simplicity. However, an ascetic lifestyle can be a very good and fruitful thing. In our culture of comfort, we've abandoned not only the virtue of simplicity; we've also abandoned practices like fasting.

Thomas Dubay made this point much better than I could:

> "A genteel, soft, comfortable existence is foreign to the New Testament, because for wounded men and women it is foreign to being in love. Only those can love sincerely who are entirely purified

by the Word, detached from things less than God (1 Peter 1:22–23). Saint John of the Cross writes so much about detachment because he writes so much about supreme love. Saint Paul has the same message: only on condition that we crucify all self-indulgent desires can we belong to Christ Jesus (Gal. 5:24). Hence it is no objection to revealed doctrine on factual poverty to say it is difficult and requires sacrifice. Of course. They who want no part of asceticism want no part of love."[6]

I guess by only calling for simplicity, and not asceticism, I'm just a moderate!

The lifestyle that I am living, and promoting, is not ascetic in the least. In the end, it is not austere, not really radical. It's simply a rejection of the culture of consumerism that says, "Whatever you can afford to purchase is rightfully yours." Or the slightly adapted Christian form of this premise: "Whatever you can afford to purchase after giving away ten percent of your income is rightfully yours." Because I have rejected those premises and opted instead to live simply, with an attitude of sparing and sharing, I find that I live in a smaller house with less expensive clothes and simpler food than I otherwise would…but I never go without.

---

[6] Thomas Dubay, *Happy Are You Poor: The Simple Life and Spiritual Freedom* (San Francisco: Ignatius Press, 1981), 42.

I had to explain this to my daughter, Lucia. She was commenting that our house is not as nice or as big as any of her friends' or cousins' houses. And yet she was aware that it was much, much bigger than the houses that many—possibly even most—people in the world live in. I explained that we had to seek balance: that in Kenya, I saw houses that we in Canada would regard as unsuitable to be used even as sheds, and though in theory we could live in such a building and give more to the poor, both discernment and an informed conscience are needed.

I am not endorsing an asceticism beyond what God calls us to in the Bible. Let us consider the standard to which St. Paul actually challenged the Corinthians:

> "Our desire is not that others might be relieved while you are hard pressed, but that there might be equality. At the present time your plenty will supply what they need, so that in turn their plenty will supply what you need. The goal is equality, as it is written: "The one who gathered much did not have too much, and the one who gathered little did not have too little." (2 Corinthians 8:13–15)

What standard do we go for? I'm just aiming for equality. I sometimes wonder if everyone in the world could conceivably live at the standard that I am living at. Frankly, I doubt it. I'm still living in too much luxury. Unjust governments and corruption aside, I do not believe the world has sufficient resources or that it can withstand the impact of the entire earth's population living as I do. I have further yet to go.

But by the standard I have set, my family will continue to enjoy small vacations, always have enough clothes to wear, and will eat decent meals—but we can make do with eating meat less often each week, with wearing secondhand clothing, and with camping vacations near home. My lifestyle is far from ascetic, and I know that I am not even close to living at a heroic or radical level. But I hope it is approaching consistency with scripture.

The Deceitfulness of Wealth

Scripture is abundantly clear that wealth can be a major obstacle in a person's relationship with Christ. Interestingly, our Blessed Mother seems to celebrate this fact as a feature of God's justice in the Magnificat, which echoes Hannah's song in 1 Samuel 2:2–8.

In her Magnificat (Luke 1:46–55), Mary says, "He has cast down the mighty from their thrones but has lifted up the lowly. He has filled the hungry with good things, but the rich He has sent away empty" (Luke 1:52–53). She appears to be rejoicing about this. I find that strange, being one of the rich who will be sent away empty. But again, this is consistent with many other scripture passages about wealth.

Jesus talks about it in the Sermon on the Mount when He contrasts the woes of the rich with the blessedness of the poor:

- "Woe to you who are rich, for you have received your comfort." (Luke 6:24)

- "Blessed are you who are poor, for yours is the kingdom of God." (Luke 6:20)

Perhaps the strongest passage in this regard comes to us from St. James. Remember, James is the one who warned us that "faith without works is dead" (James 2:17). Is our faith then dead if we do not respond to his warning to the rich?

> "Now listen, you rich people, weep and wail because of the misery that is coming on you. Your wealth has rotted, and moths have eaten your clothes. Your gold and silver are corroded. Their corrosion will testify against you and eat your flesh like fire. You have hoarded wealth in the last days. Look! The wages you failed to pay the workers who mowed your fields are crying out against you. The cries of the harvesters have reached the ears of the Lord Almighty. You have lived on earth in luxury and self-indulgence. You have fattened yourselves in the day of slaughter."
> (James 5:1–5)

Or consider the Parable of the Rich Fool in Luke 12:16–21. He puts all his grain in barns, saving up for the future, before dying and losing it all, when God says, "You fool!" Jesus sums it up by saying, "This is how it will be for whoever stores up things for themselves but is not rich towards God." I wonder: are we in the West not doing what is foolish in the sight of God?

In Ezekiel 34, the prophet describes the fat sheep that eat the food and drink the water before trampling the food and muddy the water of the lean sheep. God says to these fat sheep: "The sleek and strong I will destroy" (Ezekiel 34:16). It is hard to imagine a time in history when it was not more true than now that the rich ate and drank while wasting food and polluting the water of the poor.

Why is scripture so hard on the rich? Does God hate them? Of course not. But in the Christian order, it is apparent that wealth is often a source of woe and not of blessings. We will discuss this at length in a later chapter.

Lovers of Money

One of my favourite passages about this subject is 1 Timothy 6:10: "The love of money is the root of all evil." It's always nice when scripture gives you a handy soundbite that sums up a whole argument. Whenever this passage comes up, however, people merely point out that the passage does not say that money is the root of evil but rather that the *love* of money is.

I don't know exactly what people think a lover of money is. Maybe they imagine Donald Duck's uncle, Scrooge McDuck, diving into his piles of gold coins as if they were a pool of water, and swimming in his vaults. (If you think about it, that would actually really hurt, and that kind of love of money would also be the root of every kind of injury!)

But someone might say, "I possess money; it does not possess me." Fair enough. But it seems obvious to me that being a lover of money means living in luxury while others go without.

Whoever loves money never has enough;

> "Whoever loves wealth is never satisfied with their income. This too is meaningless. As goods increase, so do those who consume them. And what benefit are they to the owners except to feast their eyes on them? The sleep of a labourer is sweet, whether they eat little or much, But as for the rich, their abundance permits them no sleep."
> (Ecclesiastes 5:10–12)

If you agree that most North Americans fit the bill of "lovers of money," be advised that scripture warns against this over and over, in passages such as Luke 16:14, 1 Timothy 3:2–3, and Hebrews 13:5. In fact, in his second letter to Timothy, St. Paul even suggests that this quality will be one of the awful qualities that will characterize the people of the last days.

> "But mark this: there will be terrible times in the last days. People will be lovers of themselves, lovers of money, boastful, proud, abusive, disobedient to their parents, ungrateful, unholy…" (2 Timothy 3:1–2)

I'll leave the speculation to others as to whether these are the last days.

St. Paul tells us we should flee from the love of money (1 Timothy 6:11). That word "flee" reminds me of a sermon I once heard that contrasted the temptation of Joseph in the Old Testament when he was seduced by Potiphar's wife (Genesis 39) with that of David when he saw Bathsheba bathing on the rooftop (2 Samuel 11). While David looks a second time and so is seduced and led into sin, Joseph flees from temptation and so remains undefiled. Likewise, St. Paul tells us to flee the seduction of money.

Yet even if someone disputes the interpretation of the phrase "lover of money" to try to justify living in luxury, surely we can all agree that we are being greedy when we put our own wasteful desires before meeting the needs of others.

Consider this passage from the St. Paul's first letter to the Corinthians:

> "But now I am writing to you that you must not associate with anyone who claims to be a brother or sister but is sexually immoral or *greedy,* an idolater

or slanderer, a drunkard or swindler. Do not even eat with such people." (1 Corinthians 5:11, emphasis mine)

You can find other lists like this in 1 Corinthians 6:9–10, Ephesians 5:5, and Colossians 3:5. These passages tell us that we should not associate with greedy people, that greedy people will not inherit the kingdom of God, and that we should put to death any greed in our own lives. According to Ephesians and Colossians, greed is idolatry.

So, if we are greedy, should we be excommunicated? Are we in danger of Hell? Frighteningly, this theme is repeated throughout the New Testament. This is one of those moments where scripture seems to be saying much more than I want to say, but I think it is worth mentioning.

Let us heed Christ's warning: "Watch out! Be on your guard against all kinds of greed; a man's life does not consist in the abundance of his possessions." (Luke 12:15)

You Cannot Serve God and Money

It is commonly believed that when Jesus said, "You cannot serve God and Mammon" in Luke 16:13 that Mammon was a reference to some pagan deity or demon who was worshipped in the Ancient Near East. However, this appears to be a medieval interpretation of the text, since the word Jesus used was the Aramaic word "mammon," meaning "riches" or "wealth." Why does He keep coming back to this dichotomy? Is it really either-or?

There are many, many verses in the Bible that tell us that we are to be "in the world but not of the world" (cf. John 17:15–16) and that "what people value highly is detestable in God's sight" (Luke 16:15). It is apparent then that our value system as Christians should reject the things of the world—but what are these things? Too often our morality gets reduced to sins of sensuality, so we think that to be "in the world but not of it" means to be chaste and not on drugs or getting (too) drunk. But we are also supposed to be humble and not aspiring to power, modest as opposed to vain, and so on. Frankly we are to find detestable many of the things that everyone else around us values. Are we living as a contradiction to our culture and transforming it in the process, or are we instead conforming to it? (cf. Romans 12:2)

James tells us that our faith is dead if we do not meet the needs of our brothers and sisters (James 2:14–17). John tells us that God's love does not abide in us if we close our hearts to the needy. (1 John 3:17–18)

I believe that when Christ says you cannot serve God and money, what He means is that you cannot serve God and money. As in, you actually can't. The two are simply not compatible. Why not? Maybe the parable of the sower can shed some light on this. You know the parable: a man goes out to sow some seed; some seed falls on the path, some among thorns, some in good soil, etc. Jesus explains that the seed is the Word that should bear fruit in our lives. But listen to this warning: "The seed falling among the thorns refers to someone who hears the Word, but the worries of this life and the deceitfulness of wealth choke the Word, making it unfruitful." (Matthew 13:22)

It is clear from scripture that seeking holiness is incompatible with seeking wealth.

The Model of Christ and the Early Church

To be a disciple is something different from being a student. A student learns from his teacher, whereas a disciple seeks to become like his master. Therefore the argument that we are to live simply could also be made from the fact that Jesus Himself was poor. We know this in part because His parents offered a sacrifice of two young doves in Luke 2:24, which according to Leviticus 12:8 was the offering expected of households that could not afford a lamb. Jesus spoke of His own poverty when He said, "Foxes have dens and birds have nests, but the Son of Man has no place to lay His head." (Matthew 8:20).

Now again, He was not living in destitution. His tunic was a nice seamless one, worth gambling over. He ate and provided for others. It is traditionally believed that He followed His earthly father Joseph in his carpentry trade. But it is clear that He did not live in wealth (although He did experience a luxurious baby shower. I wonder what he did with His gold, frankincense and myrrh?).

Jesus' first disciples lived in imitation of their Master. It is clear that the early Church was a community that made sacrifices and took care of the poor, and in fact the appointment of the first deacons took place so that someone would have the responsibility of caring for the poor and the widows to free the Apostles to preach. (See Acts 6:1–4, Acts 4:32–37, and Acts 5:1–5.)

We too ought to imitate the Master and live like the disciple—to live simply in order to help the poor.

Old Testament Broken Covenant

In both the Old and the New Testaments, caring for the poor is a part of what it means to be God's people in covenant with Him. In the Old Testament, caring for the poor was codified in laws and in institutions such as the Jubilee Year, which involved a redistribution of wealth and property every fifty years.

Ever since I was a child, I heard that the exile in Babylon—when Jerusalem was destroyed and the Jews deported—was a result of idolatry on the part of the Israelites. This was, of course, on account of the Israelites seeming to follow this vicious cycle of receiving God's blessings, turning away from God and to idols, having the blessings removed, and then turning back to God again. But part of their failure in keeping their part of the covenant was also that they did not keep the Jubilee Year or care for the poor in their midst.

You can read about this in Amos when he warns those in the Northern Kingdom about their impending doom:

> "You lie on beds adorned with ivory
> and lounge on your couches.
> You dine on choice lambs
> and fattened calves...
> You drink wine by the bowlful
> and use the finest lotions,
> but you do not grieve over the ruin of Joseph.
> Therefore, you will be among the first to go into exile; your feasting and lounging will end."
> (Amos 6:4, 6–7)

You'll find similar warnings to the people of Judah from Isaiah (Isaiah 10:1–3, 1:23–24, 3:15–26), Micah (Micah 2:2–3) and Ezekiel, who compares Judah to Sodom and says that Sodom was destroyed in part because of its pathetic treatment of the poor:

> "Now this was the sin of your sister Sodom: She and her daughters were arrogant, overfed and unconcerned; they did not help the poor and needy. They were haughty and did detestable things before me. Therefore, I did away with them as you have seen." (Ezekiel 16: 49–50)

Jeremiah too takes up the cause of the poor in Jeremiah 7:5–7 and Jeremiah 22:13–19 where he warns King Jehoiakim and the people of Judah what would happen unless they repented of their injustice. This prophetic warning was fulfilled in 587 BC when Jerusalem was captured, and the people of Judah were taken into exile in Babylon. As for King Jehoiakim, he was first made a vassal and later died in disgrace (it is believed by assassination), and his body thrown outside the city walls.

Jeremiah's words on this are particularly haunting:

> "Among my people are the wicked…
> they have become rich and powerful
> and have grown fat and sleek.
> Their evil deeds have no limit;
> they do not seek justice.
> They do not promote the case of the fatherless;
> they do not defend the just cause of the poor.
> Should I not punish them for this?"
> declares the Lord.
> "Should I not avenge myself
> on such a nation as this?" (Jeremiah 5:26–29)

Salvation Issue?

In the Old Covenant, failure to keep the covenant meant exile, the removal of blessings, and the destruction of Jerusalem and of the temple. But what about the New Covenant? The promise of the New Covenant is that we would be adopted as sons and daughters of God and enjoy eternal life with Him. If injustice towards the poor is so serious an offence, are we in danger of missing out on our inheritance?

It is with trepidation that I broach this subject. I seriously considered just overlooking this whole concept. They say that you can interpret scripture to say what you want it to say. Well, I truly hate to think that North American Christians living in luxury, while others go without, may be in danger of losing their salvation—especially since so many of them are living lives that are otherwise godly in every respect. And of course, if anyone should feel judged or condemned by me, they might just turn around and say to me, "All right, what makes you think *you're* making the cut?"

My answer to that question? I don't know. Should I have confident assurance of my hope (cf. Hebrews 11:1) or should I be working out my own salvation in fear and trembling (cf. Philippians 2:12)? On the one hand, I want to trust in God's immeasurable mercy and grace; on the other hand, I don't want to presume upon it. God is a God both of mercy and of justice.

There is a much wider debate in the Christian world over whether we are saved "by faith" or "by works." Many people who are familiar with this debate realize that this is in fact a false dichotomy, and I will address the subject briefly later. For now, however, let it be said that those who maintain that all we need to do is declare that "Jesus is Lord" and we will be saved regardless of our works are holding a belief that is in direct contradiction to Matthew 7:21: "Not everyone who says to Me 'Lord, Lord' will enter the Kingdom of Heaven, but only the one who does the will of my Father."

Salvation is a process, a process of sanctification by grace through Christ, but we must cooperate with that grace and allow it to make us holy. A failure to accept God's sanctifying grace is a failure to accept His salvation. It is imperative then that we allow God to make us holy in every respect, including with regards to our finances.

We have explored earlier how you cannot serve God and money, that pursuing holiness is incompatible with pursuing wealth, and that failure to care for the poor is a covenant-breaker. Jesus emphasized this further when He taught about how difficult it was for a rich person to enter Heaven: "It is easier for a camel to pass through the eye of a needle than for someone who is rich to enter the kingdom of God" (Matthew 19:24; cf. Mark 10:24–27 and Luke 18:24–27).

It is important to note, however, that Jesus does qualify this by saying, "With man this is impossible, but with God all things are possible" (Matthew 19:27). But I don't think we can therefore dismiss this warning. For Jesus, the road to life is narrow and hard, and the road to destruction is wide and easy (Matthew 7:13–14). I am afraid that far too often we choose to take the easy road: "Those who want to get rich fall into temptation and a trap and into many foolish and harmful desires that plunge people into ruin and destruction" (1 Timothy 6:9).

Consider the parable of the rich man and Lazarus, found in Luke 16:19–31, where the rich man is tormented in Hades because he "lived in luxury every day" and did nothing for Lazarus. Will we fare any better simply because the poor do not live at our very doors, but a few blocks away, out of sight?

Remember that at the judgment, Jesus will separate the sheep from the goats on the basis of whether we fed the little ones when they were hungry or gave them drink when they were thirsty or clothes when they were naked. Those who did not—the goats—will go to eternal punishment (cf. Matthew 25:31–46). When you couple these teachings of Christ with the dire warnings in the writings of St. Paul that the greedy will not inherit the kingdom (1 Corinthians 6:9–10; cf. 1 Corinthians 5:11, Ephesians 5:5, and Colossians 3:5), it paints a pretty bleak picture.

Like any of you, I hope and pray that I and all my loved ones will be with God in the beatific vision, and I know that God's mercy is greater than mine, that His goodness and His love is greater than mine. But at the same time, I also know that fear of the Lord is the beginning of wisdom (Proverbs 9:10), and I think it would be very unwise to ignore the call of scripture to repentance.

What Can We Conclude from Scripture?

To sum up, Catholic apologist and speaker Dr. Timothy Gray put it this way: "Social justice, our relationship with the poor, is not one small piece of the puzzle, but frames the entire mosaic of scripture."[7]

---

[7] Gray, *Encountering the Poor.*

Scripture is clearly teaching the following things:

- If we are to be Christ's disciples, we should seek to imitate Him and to be made holy through Him.
- Love of money is incompatible with love of God, and the pursuit of wealth is incompatible with the pursuit of holiness.
- God is very concerned with our treatment of the poor, and to disregard them may be endangering our salvation.
- Wealth is deceitful and a snare that prevents the Word of God from bearing fruit in our lives.
- We therefore ought to live simply in order to be more generous with the poor.
- God will richly reward us for our generosity and will not be outdone.

It seems overwhelming to me how frequently scripture deals with this issue and seems to affirm the conclusions that, if applied today, means that a great many of us need to repent and ask for mercy.

But what assurance do I have that I am interpreting these passages correctly? There are Christians who preach the "prosperity gospel" based on passages such as Proverbs 15:6 ("In the house of the righteous there is much treasure") and Malachi 3:10–12 (that says that if we tithe, God will "pour out so much blessing that there will not be room enough to store it").

Their message is essentially to serve God and trust Him (often by giving a considerable amount to the preacher who is saying to do so), and He will bless you with wealth.

Which interpretation is correct? How can we know?

I give my assent of faith to the Catholic Church. When Christ gave the Apostles the authority "to bind and to loose" (Matthew 18:18), and when St. Paul told the Ephesians that pastors and Apostles were given to us to keep us from "being tossed to and fro...with every wind of doctrine" (cf. Ephesians 4:11–14), these passages point to the authority of the Church to interpret scripture and to teach authoritatively on matters of faith and morals. So, are my conclusions consistent with the teachings of the Catholic Church? That will be the subject of our next chapter.

Chapter Three Discussion Questions

1. They say that when you buy a certain kind of vehicle, you suddenly start noticing it everywhere. Now that you are thinking more about submitting your finances to God's will, have you noticed it addressed more in scripture?

2. "Anyone who has two shirts should share with the one who has none, and anyone who has food should do the same." John the Baptist, Luke 3:11. Consider your wardrobe. Would a contemporary John the Baptist tell you that you need to repent?

3. "Give until it hurts"- Attributed to Mother Teresa. Do you think Christians are giving until it hurts, or are they more likely to give out of their excess? (Cf. Mark 12:41-44)

4. "They who want no part of asceticism want no part of love." Thomas Dubay. Are you repelled or attracted to asceticism, the avoidance of all forms of indulgence?

5. St Paul wrote "The goal is equality" (Cf 2 Corinthians 8:13-15). Suppose everyone in the world lived the way you do. Would that be sustainable? Economically? Ecologically? What changes would we have to make to start living sustainably?

6. Scripture is often harsh on the rich: "The rich he has sent away empty." (Luke 1:53); "Woe to you who are rich" (Luke 6:24); "Now listen, you rich people, weep and wail for the misery that is coming on you." (James 5:1). Just to cite a few. When you hear scripture rebuking the rich, do you feel convicted, or do you tend to think that those words are directed at someone else?

7. Scripture warns us repeatedly against being a 'lover of money' or 'greedy.' In fact, we are to 'flee' from the love of money (Cf. 1 Timothy 6:11). What does it mean to be a lover of money? Can you live in luxury and enjoy excess wealth without developing an inordinate desire for money?

8. "You cannot serve God and money", Jesus, Luke 16:13. Was Jesus exaggerating? Even if He was, and someone argues that it is possible to serve both God and money, is it prudent?

9. Before reading this chapter, were you aware that neglect of the poor was one of the themes that prophets returned to when they warned Israel that they were not being faithful to their covenant with God?

10. Do you think the way we spend our money is a salvation issue?

Chapter Four
Church Teaching

If you want to know what the Catholic Church teaches on a topic, the best place to look is in the *Catechism of the Catholic Church*, published in 1992. Unlike the Bible, which was not written to either outline dogmas or define morals, the *Catechism* was written for precisely those purposes. Of course, if you want a really in-depth study on anything, the *Catechism* is insufficient, but if you want a summary of the Church's teachings on a matter, it's always the first place to go.

I think it was my wife who first discovered the Church's teachings on this subject. It was during that period in our lives where we were already living with the discipline of the luxury budget and increasingly living more simply, but we just thought it was "our own thing" rather than a Church teaching for everybody. When Catherine and I were asked to be the keynote speakers at a Lenten retreat for university students, we took for our structure the obvious themes of prayer, fasting, and almsgiving.

As Catherine was doing her research on almsgiving, she stumbled across the section in the *Catechism* that addresses the Catholic teachings on social justice. The *Catechism* is divided into four main parts, the third of which is "Life in Christ," which uses the traditional Ten Commandments as its template in discussing Catholic moral principles. For example, it addresses all manner of sexual morality under the heading, "You shall not commit adultery" (2331–2400). Similarly, it addresses a lot of the Church's teachings on social justice under the heading, "You shall not steal" (2401–2463).

If you really want to explore this idea, I recommend reading through that whole section of the *Catechism*. You will find the teaching both stronger and more specific than what I will cover here. But rather than just reproducing that section, I will point to some highlights and to some other sources as well that reinforce the universal call to simplicity.

According to the *Catechism*, "The Social Doctrine of the Church developed in the nineteenth century when the Gospel encountered modern industrial society."[8] There is a set of papal encyclicals (letters from popes) commonly accepted to be the official Catholic social teaching documents. They began with *Rerum Novarum* in 1891, and the unofficial set contains some thirteen encyclicals, as well as other documents written by popes and bishops.

Not all the encyclicals deal with the matter we are discussing, and so when you read the *Catechism*, you will find an emphasis on things such as the right to private ownership of goods (in response to communism), the dignity and rights of workers, and teaching responding to the major ethical questions that arose during the last century. There are many who have interpreted the early Church's model of sharing wealth

---

[8] *Catechism of the Catholic Church (CCC)* (New York: Doubleday, 1994), 2421.

and holding everything in common as a form of communism, but unlike communism, both the Church and scripture affirm an individual's right to private property. As tends to be the case with Church teaching, she does not wholeheartedly endorse a particular economic or political structure. Often when we are suspicious of one of the Church's teachings, our suspicion has more to do with our political bias than with our faith, so it is important to remember that the Church is neither politically left nor right but promotes the truth and so often affirms values from both sides or neither side of our political spectrum.

While the Church clearly affirms the right to private property, she warns us of the abuses associated with this right: "The right to private property is not absolute and unconditional. No one may appropriate surplus goods solely for his own private use when others lack the bare necessities of life."[9]

Read that quote from Pope Paul VI again. It kind of sums up the whole teaching, doesn't it? "No one is authorized to reserve for their exclusive use what he does not need, when others lack necessities." What I discovered from reading what the Church teaches is that we don't even have the *right* to live in luxury while others go without. I had based my decision to live simply on the ideas that it was the loving thing to do and that I must love my neighbour as myself. And of

---

[9] Paul VI, *Populorum Progressio* (1967 Encyclical), s.23, retrieved from http://www.vatican.va/content/paul-vi/en/encyclicals/documents/hf_p-vi_enc_26031967_populorum.html.

course, love is a superior motivator than duty or fear. But as we will see, the Church's teaching is that living simply is in fact a moral duty to which we are bound.

I often liken this to the Church's teaching on contraception. Ideally we would value life and love children and the full theological significance of the sexual act so much that we would not use contraception. If our consciences were so perfectly formed, then we could indeed obey our consciences without watering down the teaching. But since we are by and large so poorly catechized, our consciences are ill-formed, and many of us obey that directive out of obedience rather than love. But our obedience to this hard teaching does change our hearts so that we begin to understand the teaching.

Perhaps if we are not sufficiently charitable to embrace simplicity out of love, we will at least embrace it out of obedience to the Church's social teaching.

Of course, the tradition of the Catholic Church in regard to justice and charity goes back much further than *Rerum Novarum*. Pope Saint John Paul II wrote on the 100th anniversary of *Rerum Novarum* that "the Church's love for the poor…[is] a part of her constant tradition."[10]

At the heart of Catholic social teaching is this love of the poor. The *Catechism* teaches us that God "blesses

---

[10] John Paul II, *Centesimus Annus* (1991 Encyclical Letter), s.57, retrieved from http://www.vatican.va/content/john-paul-ii/en/encyclicals/documents/hf_jp-ii_enc_01051991_centesimus-annus.html.

those who come to the aid of the poor and rebukes those who turn away from them"[11] and in fact makes the point that Jesus will recognize His chosen ones by the way they treat the poor, referring to Matthew 25:31–36 where Jesus discusses the separation of the sheep from the goats.

Love of the poor is a defining characteristic of what it means to be a disciple. You cannot be a disciple if you do not love the poor any more than you can be a disciple if you do not love God, because you cannot love God if you do not love others (1 John 4:20).

The Universal Destination of Goods

The Church teaches the principle of the Universal Destination of Goods, meaning that "God gave the earth to the whole human race for the sustenance of all its members, without excluding or favouring anyone."[12]

St. John Paul II called the Universal Destination of Goods "the first principle of the whole ethical and social order"[13] and "the characteristic principle of Catholic social doctrine."[14]

---

[11] *CCC*, 2443.

[12] Canadian Conference of Catholic Bishops (CCCB), *Compendium of the Social Doctrine of the Church* (Ottawa: CCCB Publications, 2005), 171.

[13] John Paul II, *Laborem Exercens* (1981 Encyclical), s.19, retrieved from http://www.vatican.va/content/john-paul-ii/en/encyclicals/documents/hf_jp-ii_enc_14091981_laborem-exercens.html.

[14] John Paul II, *Sollicitudo Rei Socialis* (1987 Encyclical Letter), s.42,

In other words, everything the Church teaches regarding money hinges on this principle. According to it, every human should "have access to the level of well-being necessary for his full development."[15] Where there is no access to these needs, there is an ethical imperative to provide access.

When Jesus says to "love your neighbour as yourself," isn't it obvious that this means we should give our neigbour enough to not only survive, but to thrive? And if we must sacrifice the things that we know are luxuries, that are beyond what is needed for our own "full development"—well, after all, isn't that what love is?

More Than Charity: The Demands of Justice

The Church is very clear in her teaching on this matter. In fact, the Church goes further than I originally expected her to. I expected to discover an exhortation to love, to perform the traditional corporal works of mercy—you know, feed the hungry, clothe the naked, shelter the homeless—that kind of thing. I find exhortations to love to resonate at a certain level and can be inspiring, but often when I hear them, I nod my head and think, "Yeah, that would be nice." But to my surprise, the Church considers these actions not only as charity but as demanded by justice.

retrieved from http://www.vatican.va/content/john-paul-ii/en/encyclicals/documents/hf_jp-ii_enc_30121987_sollicitudo-rei-socialis.html.

[15] *Compendium*, 172.

The *Catechism* makes the case quite strongly:

2445 Love for the poor is incompatible with immoderate love of riches or their selfish use:

> Come now, you rich, weep and howl for the miseries that are coming upon you. Your riches have rotted and your garments are moth-eaten. Your gold and silver have rusted, and their rust will be evidence against you and will eat your flesh like fire. You have laid up treasure for the last days. Behold, the wages of the labourers who mowed your fields, which you kept back by fraud, cry out; and the cries of the harvesters have reached the ears of the Lord of hosts. You have lived on the earth in luxury and in pleasure; you have fattened your hearts in a day of slaughter. You have condemned, you have killed the righteous man; he does not resist you.

2446 St. John Chrysostom vigorously recalls this: "Not to enable the poor to share in our goods is to steal from them and deprive them of life. The goods we possess are not ours, but theirs." "The demands of justice must be satisfied first of all; that which is already due in justice is not to be offered as a gift of charity."

Then the *Catechism* adds this quote from St. Gregory the Great: "When we attend to the needs of those in want, we give them what is theirs, not ours. More than performing works of mercy, we are paying a debt of justice."

The Church is saying here that far from loving our neighbour as ourselves, we who are living in "luxury and comfort" are actually indebted to them by justice. The principle of the Universal Destination of Goods demands that we share with the poor and provide for their needs as a bare minimum.

This is what justice means: to render to each what belongs to them.[16]

Thou Shalt Not Steal

Think again about that quote from St. Gregory the Great: "We give them what is theirs, not ours." If the Universal Destination of Goods says that the goods we have are theirs, and not ours, but we keep them for ourselves, does this imply that we are stealing from the poor? Is this why this section of the *Catechism* falls under the title, "You shall not steal"?

Servant of God Dorothy Day said, "If you have two coats, you've stolen one from the poor." This is in reference to Luke 3:11, where John the Baptist says, "If you have two coats, give one away." Do a quick inventory in your mind. How many coats do you have? How many pairs of shoes?

---

[16] Thomas Slater, "Justice," in *The Catholic Encyclopedia*, Vol. 8 (New York: Robert Appleton Company, 1910), retrieved November 15, 2015 from http://www.newadvent.org/cathen/08571c.htm.

This is also reminiscent with something that St. Basil the Great said in the fourth century: "The bread which you hold back belongs to the hungry; the coat, which you guard in your locked storage-chests, belongs to the naked."[17] And in another place he said, "By a certain wily artifice of the devil, countless pretexts of expenditure are proposed to the rich."[18] St. Basil is also the person Pope Francis was echoing when he called unbridled consumerism "the dung of the devil."[19]

Even when you embrace simplicity for the sake of the poor, you may notice that Basil's words are true: "countless pretexts of expenditure are proposed to the rich." I need this renovation done. I need this vacation. I need to provide this entertainment for my family. There is always another thing to spend money on which feels justifiable, while the poor continue to starve.

Matter of Salvation?

Do you remember this haunting question from the scripture section: am I in danger of Hell for this? I mean, whether I am or not, fear of Hell is hardly a good

---

[17] St. Basil the Great, "Homily on the saying of the *Gospel According to Luke,* 'I will pull down my barns and build bigger ones,' and on greed," s.7, retrieved from https://bekkos.wordpress.com/2009/10/08/st-basil-on-stealing-from-the-poor/.

[18] St. Basil the Great, "Sermon to the Rich," s.2, retrieved from http://stjohngoc.org/st-basil-the-greats-sermon-to-the-rich/.

[19] Francis I, "Angelus," September 22, 2019, retrieved from http://www.vatican.va/content/francesco/en/angelus/2019/documents/papa-francesco_angelus_20190922.html.

reason to start acting charitably, or, as it turns out, justly. Nonetheless, it did seem to be the clear implication of a number of scripture passages.

You may put your mind at ease on this matter. Nowhere in the *Catechism* under "You shall not steal" does it say we are in danger of damnation for failing to meet our duties to the poor. And we're clear under "You shall not covet" (2534–2557), too…unless you consider paragraph 2544, where it says, "detachment from riches is obligatory for entrance into the Kingdom of Heaven." But, I mean, that can be easily overlooked.

Just make sure you don't look under the heading "Hell" (1033), where it says, "Our Lord warns us that we shall be separated from Him if we fail to meet the serious needs of the poor and the little ones who are his brethren."

Mortal and Venial Sins

I know I am making light of a very serious and frightening prospect here; call it a defense mechanism. I am actually quite uncomfortable with this prospect because of its implications for me and for the many Christians I know who love God and the Church and yet are living in luxury while others go without in clear violation of our duties.

If scripture and the Church are clear that living in luxury at least endangers our salvation, it would behoove us to listen. But we like to think to ourselves, "No, it can't be. God loves me too much, and I'm basically a good person."

The best analogy to understand our relationship with God is that it is like a marriage. As in marriage, we are committed to love and honour one another, and in our relationship with God, we know that He will always be faithful. But as in marriage, there are certain things that we can do that are deal-breakers. If I am unfaithful to my wife, I can hope that she will forgive me. But if I am unfaithful to my wife and am unrepentant? This is a deal-breaker.

What if my wife left for a few days, and I was responsible to care for my children. After three days she returns and finds the children crying and sick because for three days I did not feed them. Suppose she says to me, "Why didn't you feed them?"

I shrug and respond, "I spent all the money on beer and entertainment."

She says, "Did you not hear them crying?"

I reply, "I did at first, but I was able to tune them out with beer and entertainment."

Any sensible person would agree that whether we are technically divorced or not, our relationship is at that moment terminated.

Well, what of our relationship with God when we let His children go hungry while we go on luxury cruises? God is merciful, but God is also just. Have we lost our fear of God "who, after killing the body, has the power to throw you into Hell"? (Luke 12:5)

The Hunger Games is a fictional dystopian series in which the majority of people live in poverty while the minority in the Capital live in wealth and luxury, not only having their fill but also wasting food and resources. When we watch the movies or read the books, we are meant to feel a sense of moral outrage at the people in the Capital.

Well, in a certain sense, *we* are the Capital. And greed is a capital sin—one of the seven deadly sins. When Thomas Aquinas defends its status as one of the deadly sins, he points out that it is a sin against ourselves, a sin against God, and a sin against our neighbour: "On this way it is a sin directly against one's neighbour, since

one man cannot over-abound in external riches, without another man lacking them."[20]

But if the question is, "are Christians who live in luxury in danger of Hell?" the answer is, "it depends on their formation." This is because of the Church's teaching on mortal and venial sins: "I refer to those whose sin does not lead to death. There is a sin that leads to death.... All wrongdoing is sin, and there is sin that does not lead to death" (1 John 5:16–17).

This distinction between sin that leads to death and sin that does not is what the Church calls "mortal sin" and "venial sin." While we should avoid all sins—even the

[20] Thomas Aquinas, *Summa Theologiae*, II-II, Q. 118, Art. 1. ad 2, translated by the Fathers of the English Dominican Province

small "venial" ones—it is the mortal ones that by definition threaten our salvation. A mortal sin is one that cuts us off from the life of God.

There is much dispute about how you actually know when a sin crosses from venial to mortal. I think it is possible that any sin, if done in extreme measure, can become a mortal sin.

For a sin to be mortal, the following conditions must apply:

1. It must be grave matter.

2. You must have full knowledge that it is a serious sin.

3. You must have full consent to the sin.

4. You do it anyway.

I would like to suggest that the way in which we tend to spend our money selfishly while others go without— what the Church calls stealing from the poor—is a grave matter. This is why so many scripture verses tell us that we are endangering our salvation, or that love of money is incompatible with love of God. Simply put, it cuts us off from the life of God.

I am not alone in thinking this. Thomas Dubay makes the same point in his book *Happy Are You Poor: The Simple Life and Spiritual Freedom*. He notes that you can find the prohibition against living in luxury while others go without in the writings of Luke, Paul, and

James, and then he says this:

> "The Johannine tradition bears the same
> blunt message: if a person of means sees
> a needy disciple but closes his heart
> tohim, that person cannot be loving God.
> Apparently, we have here a serious sin
> which destroys the life of grace.[21]

I suppose that we can hope that our ignorance of this principle has excused us thus far from living according to it. It is a grave sin, but we can hope that it is not mortal.

Love, Not Fear

But as I said before, fear of Hell is a lousy reason to live by charity. After all, the call of the Gospels is to selflessness, and I think it would be counterproductive to preach selflessness for the sake of selfish motives. Serving God for the sake of fear of Hell is rather like doing the minimum requirements in marriage for the sake of fear of divorce. The point is to do things out of love.

So yes, it is a demand of justice to share our wealth with the poor, but as St. Paul says in 1 Corinthians 13:3, "If I give all I have to the poor...but do not have love, I gain nothing." John Paul II emphasized this when he said, "By itself, justice is not enough. Indeed, it can even betray itself unless it is open to that deeper power

[21] Thomas Dubay, S.M. *Happy are you Poor; The Simple Life and Spiritual Freedom,* 2003, Ignatius Press, San Francisco

which is love."[22]

So it is my hope that we will give generously to the poor, but that it would be rooted not in a sense of duty or obligation, or selfish motives like seeking rewards or fear of Hell, but rooted deeply in love of God and love for the poor.

Where Do We Draw the Line?

All of this brings me back to my crisis point in the Indian Ocean: are we really not authorized to acquire any luxury goods? Is it always selfish to do so?

Perhaps the reason that there are not more Catholics speaking on this teaching is because practically, it is not well-defined. It appears from my research that it is left largely to our own consciences to determine how much we ought to own and how much we ought to give away. The difficulty with this is that unless we have mature and well-informed consciences, our consciences may be unreliable guides.

This is why we must continue to study Church teaching on the matter.

> "In economic matters, respect for the human dignity requires the practice of the virtue of temperance, so as to moderate attachment to this world's goods, the

---

[22] John Paul II, "Message for the 2004 World Day of Peace" (January 1, 2004), s.10, retrieved from https://www.vatican.va/content/john-paul-ii/en/messages/peace/documents/hf_jp-ii_mes_20031216_xxxvii-world-day-for-peace.html.

practice of the virtue of justice, to preserve our neighbour's rights and render him what is his due: the practice of solidarity, in accordance with the Golden Rule."[23]

Here again we find the vague term "moderate" and are left to our consciences to determine what is moderate and what is not.

On the one hand, the Church teaches that economic development is good, provided it is in keeping with social justice,[24] and that economic activity can be a response to our vocation and can even be a place of sanctification.[25] This was the major focus of the work of St. Josemaría Escrivá, founder of Opus Dei (Latin for "work of God"), who said, "We see in work a means of perfection, a way to sanctity."[26]

This is important, in case someone thinks that living simply means they should give up their high-paying employment as a doctor or a lawyer or a businessman. On the contrary, it is suitable for Catholics to pursue these high-paying and influential jobs, and we should recognize the wealth that flows from them as a blessing. I like how Randy Alcorn puts it: "Too often we assume that God has increased our income to increase our

[23] *CCC*, 2407.

[24] *CCC*, 2426.

[25] *Compendium*, 326.

[26] Escrivá de Balaguer, *Conversations with Monsignor Escrivá de Balaguer,* 2nd ed. (Dublin: Ecclesia Press, Dublin: 1972), 10.

standard of living, when His stated purpose is to increase our standard of giving."[27] Far from discouraging us from working, the Church teaches that "love for the poor is even one of the motives for the duty of working so as to be able to give to those in need."[28]

The joke in my house is that this book will be wildly successful and will become the source of immense wealth for me and my family, so that we will get rich off a book about the dangers of wealth. But of course, in keeping with the principles in this book that will never happen; any income this book might generate will be donated to the poor.

But we are not expected to be completely without possessions. Clement of Alexandria said, "How could we ever do good to our neighbour if none of us possessed anything?"[29] In Clement's homily "Who Is the Rich Man That Shall Be Saved?", he explores that question and gives hope to the wealthy that we can indeed be saved—but it is the disposition of the heart that matters. He sees riches as an instrument that can be used for righteousness by the righteous.

---

[27] Randy Alcorn, *Money, Possessions and Eternity* (Carol Stream, IL: Tyndale House Publishers: 2003)

[28] *CCC*, 2444

[29] Clement of Alexandria, "Who Is the Rich Man That Shall Be Saved?" in *The Ante-Nicene Fathers: The Writings of the Early Church Fathers Down to A.D. 325*, Vol. 2, Phillip Schaff et. al. trans. (Edinburgh: T&T Publishers, 1885)

This idea is repeated by John of the Cross using King David as an illustration: "Even though he was manifestly rich, he says he was poor because his will was not fixed on riches; and he thereby lived as though really poor." [30]

What is emphasized by Christ and the Church, both today and throughout her 2,000-year history, is the conversion of the heart. The Church teaches that "the disordered desire for money cannot but produce perverse effects."[31]

> Goods, even when legitimately owned, always have a universal destination; any type of improper accumulation is immoral, because it openly contradicts the universal destination assigned to all goods by the Creator.[32]

While we can have possessions, we are given these blessings by God so that we can share them with others. Just as scripture refers to greed as idolatry and warns us that we cannot serve God and money, so the Church warns us against the dangers inherent in wealth and consumerism.

---

[30] John of the Cross, *Ascent of Mount Carmel*, Bk.1, ch. 3, 123.

[31] *CCC*, 2424.

[32] *Compendium*, 328.

Pope John Paul II wrote:

> "A disconcerting conclusion about the most recent period should serve to enlighten us: side-by-side with the miseries of under development themselves unacceptable, we find ourselves up against a form of super-development, equally inadmissible, because like the former it is contrary to what is good and to true happiness. This super-development, which consists in an excessive availability of every kind of material goods for the benefit of certain social groups, easily makes people slaves of "possession" and of immediate gratification, with no other horizon than the multiplication or continual replacement of the things already owned with others still better. This is the so-called civilization of "consumption" or "consumerism," which involves so much "throwing-away" and "waste." An object already owned but now superseded by something better is discarded, with no thought of its possible lasting value in itself, nor of some other human being who is poorer.[33]

Clearly the concerns that John Paul II raised are unique

---

[33] John Paul II, *Sollicitudo Rei Socialis*, s.28.

in many ways to our own era. Never before in history have the rich been so rich, has the gap between rich and poor been so wide.

The concern of the Church is not only for justice for the poor, but also for the well-being of our own souls. If our materialism is producing "perverse effects" or making us "slaves of possession and of immediate gratification," then we require more than just repentance and a commitment to justice: we need the healing and freeing mercy of God to work in our lives.

When I wrestle with the question of how much money I can legitimately spend on myself, I just remember that I am a steward. If I had an employee and I entrusted him with a certain amount of money to accomplish a certain task, and some of that money was spent on his reasonable needs, such as meals and transportation, I would not consider that an abuse or squandering of my money. I believe God wants us to enjoy the good things in life, but in moderation.

If we remember that the money we have is not ours but has been entrusted to us by God, then we spend it generously in keeping with God's will. It seems likely to me that as we grow in holiness and union with God's will, we will have increasing confidence in spending accordingly, but we will not be putting a legalistic limit on our spiritual growth and attempt to serve God and money and allow the deceitfulness of wealth to choke the Word.

Pope Francis

While the Church's message is the message of Christ, and it is timeless, repeated throughout the centuries by saints and doctors of the Church and by popes, I think it is particularly a message for the Church of today. The election of popes is a process guided by the Holy Spirit. Consequently, the popes often have a message that is prophetic and particular to the era in which they serve.

John Paul II will always be remembered as the pope who introduced Theology of the Body, developing the Church's teaching on sexual ethics right in a period of world history where the world was going through the Sexual Revolution. Similarly, if you were to reduce Pope Benedict XVI's teaching to a single point, it might be about the importance of truth against the dangers of relativism, which again was very timely. The wisdom of both these messages continues to unfold as our culture develops.

I believe that for today we need to listen in a particular way to the messages being taught by Pope Francis. When the Vicar of Christ writes a letter intended for the whole Catholic Church, it behooves us to listen.

Pope Francis has a very particular message about wealth for our Church. Even the name he chose—Francis—he chose to honour not the Jesuit saint, Francis Xavier, who is famous for his missionary activities, but St. Francis of Assisi, who is famous for having renounced his life of luxury in order to live in solidarity with the poor. In Pope Francis' own words,

St. Francis of Assisi "brought to Christianity an idea of poverty against the luxury, pride, vanity of the civil and ecclesiastical powers of the time. He changed history."[34]

Pope Francis' message is at the heart of the Gospel message. Christ's death and resurrection, the salvation He won for us, and the gift of the Holy Spirit should all bear the fruit of interior conversion in individual Christians. The Pope of Mercy, as he is known, is emphasizing the poor and the environment again and again in his teachings. This means that it is not only the non-Christians or those who've fallen into sexual sins who need to repent; we Christians who are neglecting the poor need to repent as well.

It is not by accident that Pope Francis keeps emphasizing the need for the rich to repent, any more than it was by accident that Jesus did. There are many who reject his message. They may be doing so because they are attached to their political ideology and are defensive against anything that might sound like "leftist" rhetoric. Rather than reject the message of the pope because it is inconsistent with our previously held convictions, we ought to ask whether the Spirit is speaking through the pope, and if perhaps our previously held convictions ought to be examined.

---

[34] Brian Bethune, "Pope Francis: How the first New World pontiff could save the church," *Maclean's* (March 26, 2013), retrieved from https://www.macleans.ca/news/world/man-of-the-people-2/.

Pope Francis is the Pope of Mercy. Mercy is the fruit of repentance, and repentance is the necessary condition for our soul to receive mercy. If the message of the pontiff is consistent with that of scripture and of Church teaching, and yet inconsistent with our own values, then I dare say the time for repentance has come. Furthermore, when we pray for mercy, we should expect that with mercy will come the grace of repentance. When I hear the call to repent repeated by the pope or in scripture, I instinctively think the call is for others, trapped and blinded by their sin. But if I am ignorantly living in a way that is contrary to the Gospel, am I not also trapped and blinded by sin?

While the pope, like Christ, is ultimately concerned with the transformation of our hearts, he is also calling for a change to the systems, to the structural sins, that hinder us from living according to the principles of solidarity and the Universal Destination of Goods. "A way has to be found to enable everyone to benefit from the fruits of the earth, and not simply to close the gap between the affluent and those who must be satisfied with the crumbs falling from the table, but above all to satisfy the demands of justice, fairness and respect for every human being."[35]

Does this way imply Marxism, a complete overthrow of this system in order to root out institutional sins? That

---

[35] Francis I, "Address to Participants in the 38th Conference of the Food and Agricultural Organization of the United Nations (FAO)" (June 20, 2013), retrieved from http://www.vatican.va/content/francesco/en/speeches/2013/june/documents/papa-francesco_20130620_38-sessione-fao.html.

would be inconsistent with the Church's teaching on private ownership. If we see it as Marxism, I think we are reading the pope's comments through our political lens. No wonder that when he spoke to Congress, Pope Francis warned against every form of polarization. We need to take seriously the message of the pope and stop letting our ideological bias prevent us from recognizing our own need for conversion.

The Message of the Pope

You probably knew well before reading this that Pope Francis was championing the rights of the poor. I've compiled a number of his quotes from encyclicals, sermons, and even his twitter feed. While the infallibility of the pope—the protection given the pope through the Holy Spirit from error when teaching on matters of faith and morals—does not extend to his tweets, we ought to consider his message as being likely inspired wisdom according to which we ought to live.

Just as scripture and Church teaching express the call to universal simplicity in words stronger than I would choose, the pope does so as well. "A Christian who is too attached to riches has lost his way."[36] Pope Francis sees the disparity of wealth as a scandal:

> The times talk to us of so much poverty
> in the world and this is a scandal. Poverty
> in the world is a scandal. In a world

---

[36] Francis I, Twitter post (August 25, 2015), retrieved from https://twitter.com/pontifex/status/636091901951610880?lang=en.

> where there is so much wealth, so many
> resources to feed everyone, it is
> unfathomable that there are so many
> hungry children, that there are so many
> children without an education, so many
> poor persons. Poverty today is a cry."[37]

It is a scandal. We're always scandalized when a priest or respected person sins sexually, and rightly so. But we have an entire society of self-declared Christians ignoring the plight of the poor. I wonder how people in the future will remember this age?

> Money must serve, not rule! The Pope
> loves everyone, rich and poor alike, but he
> is obliged in the name of Christ to remind
> all that the rich must help, respect and
> promote the poor. I exhort you to generous
> solidarity and a return of economics and
> finance to an ethical approach which
> favours human beings.[38]

The pope does recognize that this personal moral sin can become, and has become, a societal problem that

---

[37] Francis I, "Address to the Students of the Jesuit Schools of Italy and Albania" (June 7, 2013), retrieved from http://www.vatican.va/content/francesco/en/speeches/2013/june/documents/papa-francesco_20130607_scuole-gesuiti.html.

[38] Francis I, *Evangelii Gaudium* (2013 Apostolic Exhortation), s.58, retrieved from http://www.vatican.va/content/francesco/en/apost_exhortations/documents/papa-francesco_esortazione-ap_20131124_evangelii-gaudium.html.

must be addressed. Indeed, when he spoke to the G8, the pope repeated his message that money must serve, not rule, and emphasized the dignity of humans, that they cannot be reduced to a cog in the machine.

> Today, the scientific community realizes what the poor have long told us: harm, perhaps irreversible harm, is being done to the ecosystem. The earth, entire peoples and individual persons are being brutally punished. And behind all this pain, death and destruction there is the stench of what Basil of Caesarea called "the dung of the devil." An unfettered pursuit of money rules. The service of the common good is left behind. Once capital becomes an idol and guides people's decisions, once greed for money presides over the entire socioeconomic system, it ruins society, it condemns and enslaves men and women, it destroys human fraternity, it sets people against one another and, as we clearly see, it even puts at risk our common home.[39]

Notice that both the environmental and poverty problems, two of the major emphasis of Francis' papacy, are rooted in the same sin: greed and consumerism. If the message was merely that we ought

[39] Francis I, "Address at the Second World Meeting of Popular Movements," Bolivia (July 9, 2015), retrieved from http://www.vatican.va/content/francesco/en/speeches/2015/july/documents/papa-francesco_20150709_bolivia-movimenti-popolari.html.

to be generous, it would be easy to congratulate ourselves for the many charities we have donated to and feel that we are being generous.

It is commonly cited that the Catholic Church does far more charitable work than any other organization in the world. But Pope Francis teaches that consumerism itself is an issue, and it is our presuppositions of consumerism which are conditioning us towards a lack of charity for the poor. "Consumerism has accustomed us to waste. But throwing food away is like stealing it from the poor and hungry."[40]

There's that "stealing" word again, by which he affirms the Church's teaching that sharing with the poor is a matter of justice, not charity.

Pope Francis is the Vicar of Christ. Again and again, he is repeating his message that he wants the Church to be poor and to be for the poor. On the one hand this is a call for the world to examine its financial structures and to seek a just system. But for us Catholics seeking to do the will of God, it is a call for us to examine our consciences and our hearts. "Lord, help us always to be more generous and closer to poor families." [41]

---

[40] Francis, Twitter post (June 7, 2013), retrieved from https://twitter.com/pontifex/status/342930680570855425?lang=en.

[41] Francis, Twitter post (August 28, 2015), retrieved from https://twitter.com/pontifex/status/637184108909625344?lang=en.

Chapter Four Discussion Questions

1. Peter was surprised to learn that living simply was something the Church taught as a moral duty, demanded by justice, rather than just an expression of love. Had you known this before? Were you surprised to learn it? When you give to the poor, do you think of it in terms of a generous act you are doing or a just act of redistributing wealth?

2. Church teaching emphasizes the right to private property, as opposed to communism. What is the difference between the model the Church recommends and communism?

3. Peter suggests that the reason we are so often suspicious of Church teachings has something to do with our political assumptions. Have you come across this in your own experience, where Catholics align themselves with a political party and then expect Church teaching to align with that party as well?

4. The principle of the Universal Destination of Goods teaches that "God gave the earth to the whole human race for the sustenance of all its members, without excluding or favouring anyone." (Compendium of Social Justice). Do you think that earth's natural resources could sustain a growing population if they were properly managed and distributed? What do

you imagine a sustainable and equitable lifestyle would look like?

5. St Basil the Great taught that "By a certain wily artifice of the devil, countless pretexts for expenditure are proposed to the rich." When you consider your expenses and whether or not you can justify whichever luxury you are discerning, do you recognize the possibility that this is in fact a temptation towards greed? Is there anything we can do practically to stop being tempted so frequently?

6. Peter wrestles with the idea that living in luxury may endanger salvation. Is he overstating his case here? Is it safe to assume that God would not allow someone to be damned for living in luxury?

7. John Paul II, in *Sollicitudo Rei Socialis*, talks about super-development which "makes people slaves of possession and of immediate gratification." Have you noticed this phenomenon among your contemporaries, or even in yourself?

8. Pope Francis said that "Poverty in the world is a scandal." Are you scandalized when you hear about Christian leaders living in luxury?

9. There are many voices objecting to the
    messages of Pope Francis. Like anyone, Pope
    Francis can be interpreted charitably or
    uncharitably. Do you agree with Peter's
    understanding that Pope Francis was chosen
    specifically for these times to be the shepherd
    and that his message of love for the poor is
    part of God's timely message for us?

Chapter Five
On Tithing

When I was in Kenya, I was frequently asked about tithing. There is a very strong tithing culture there, influenced no doubt by the many Protestant missionaries who come there and by the Kenyans' own culture. In one location, I was asked to speak about tithing by some of the leaders in the community, and I think they were frustrated by what I taught: that as Catholics, we are not bound to tithing.

Tithing is one of the Old Testament legalisms, like circumcision and abstaining from pork, which as Catholics we no longer have to do. Traditionally, people give ten percent of their gross income to the church or to charity, and this is known as giving their tithe. Pity the leaders who asked me the question hoping that I would give a strong apologetic for the tithe.

In another place, a man asked me the question this way, "I'm a poor man, and I can barely support my wife and kids. Sometimes we go without food. Am I still required to tithe?"

I told him that no, we are not required to tithe—although it remains an admirable practice. The practice of tithing is being abused at both ends. It is abused when a poor person is expected to give ten percent of their income, when by doing so, they cannot sustain their family. It is also abused when a rich person thinks ten percent is all that they should give, and after that they can pursue a consumerist life of luxury in good conscience.

Tithing is such a big question in Kenya that I must admit I am a little suspicious now of the practice of going to the developing world to do "church planting." During my first trip, a young man who played the keyboard was making conversation with me, and it quickly became apparent that he was hoping I would give him some money. I was complimenting him on his musical ability and the particular style of music they did, which is foreign here in Canada. I said, "I would love it if people in Canada could hear you play."

To which he replied, "Maybe you could pay for me and my band to all fly to Canada, and we'll put on a concert." Of course, that would have cost me several thousand dollars, so I explained to him that this was not feasible.

Undeterred, he tried another approach, "Well, I was also thinking of maybe starting my own church, but I would need some seed money…"

I apologized again, saying, "I don't believe in starting new churches where there's an existing Church. I want to build up the Church that is here."

But I realized afterwards what a good business prospect starting your own church would be. If you were moderately successful, and attracted eleven people, and they all tithed, you would be making more than the average salary. If you could build a community of thirty, forty, fifty people—each giving ten percent of their income to your Church—well, you can see how starting your own church could be very profitable.

No wonder I saw so many small, storefront churches crammed so closely together in Kenya. So now I wonder to myself when missionaries go church planting, are they going to a place where there are no churches and evangelizing the people and training them to be leaders? Or are they just planting their own brand of church in a community that is already full of struggling churches?

In case you are wondering the kind of missionary activity I was involved with, Renewal Ministries consisted in going into Catholic parishes and providing solid Catholic teaching in a place where access to information and Catholic teachers with university degrees is scarce.

Of course, churches that ask for the tithe do have a biblical basis for doing so. Consider the following passage from Malachi, where God is speaking;

> "Will a mere mortal rob God? Yet you rob me.
>
> But you ask, 'How are we robbing you?'
>
> In tithes and offerings. You are under a curse—your whole nation—because you are robbing me. Bring the whole tithe into the storehouse, that there may be food in

my house. Test me in this," says the Lord Almighty, "and see if I will not throw open the floodgates of heaven and pour out so much blessing that there will not be room enough to store it." (Malachi 3:8–10)

When I addressed this topic to the catechists in the Ngong Diocese near Nairobi, they began laughing when they heard the reference to Malachi 3:10. I had to ask why. It turns out there was a pastor in Nairobi who had been exposed as a fraud. He used this verse as the basis for performing fake "miracles" and asking for 310 Kenya shillings (about $3 USD) as a tithe to perform his miracles. He grew wealthy from the money he collected. When the exposé was aired, his reputation in Kenya was left in tatters.

This verse in Malachi not only demands the tithe but also comes with the promise that God will provide for us financially. When I challenged the popular teaching in Kenya that all should tithe, some of the catechists were bothered by the implication that promises made by God in the Old Testament would not be fulfilled in New Testament times. This of course is not my intention; I do believe that God will look after us, and that we ought to be faithful and even generous with our money and trust in His abundant goodness. In fact, Paul talks about this in the New Testament when he is encouraging the Corinthians to be generous with their money:

"So, I thought it necessary to encourage the brothers to go on ahead to you and arrange in advance for your promised gift, so that in this way it might be ready as a bountiful gift and not as an exaction. Consider this: whoever sows sparingly will also reap sparingly, and whoever sows bountifully will also reap bountifully. Each must do as already determined, without sadness or compulsion, for God loves a cheerful giver. Moreover, God is able to make every grace abundant for you, so that in all things, always having all you need, you may have an abundance for every good work." (2 Corinthians 9:5–8)

My wife believes in this so strongly that recently when finances were tight, she gave away more money than usual, trusting that God would not be outdone in generosity and that he would repair the deficit in our accounts. And it should be noted that it worked. One of the beauties of the lifestyle I am proposing is that you really do learn to trust in God, and you find that He really does bless us and take care of our needs. On the other hand, I would not readily endorse a philosophy of being generous with God so that God would reward us, but rather that we would be generous with God in faith that He will provide for our needs.

The application of this principle to the poor is difficult. Should a poor person tithe? I do not want to deny the poor the opportunity to trust in God, to be generous, and to receive his blessings which he promised to pour out on us. But at the same time, I do not think it is right to lay upon them the burden of the tithe, which we are not bound to, asking the poor to have more faith than we ourselves have. I suppose that if we really believe the principle ourselves, then we would not be reluctant to give of our own salary until we only retain for ourselves the meager wages of the poor person we are challenging, and then we ought to tithe on what remains. I'm afraid that this requires much more faith than I have, but at least I'd be living according to the principles I am teaching when I tell poor people to tithe.

Notice the emphasis in Paul's writing: he wants what we give to God to be a "bountiful gift," not an "exaction." The difficulty with the tithe is that it can become little more than a tax. Indeed, this has literally happened historically. In fact, there was an abuse in the twelfth century that allowed even princes to receive tithes in return for the protection they offered to the Church. This abuse was done away with in 1179 at the Third Council of the Lateran. If we are not careful, even a graduated tithe[42] or a luxury budget can become little more than a legalism.

Legalism, St. Paul, and the Reformation

It is this legalism, in part, that Christ was trying to free us from. This is a major theme in the writings of St. Paul, and unfortunately misinterpretations of what he said fueled the Reformation.

---

[42] The graduated tithe is the model that Ronald J. Sider presents in *Rich Christians in an Age of Hunger: Moving from Affluence to Generosity* (Nashville: Thomas Nelson, 2010). The idea is that as your income increases, your tithe increases as well.

Martin Luther's two main arguments against the Catholic Church were *sola scriptura* (meaning "the Bible alone" is the source of truth, so we don't need the Church to interpret it for us), and *sola fide* (that "faith alone" is sufficient for our salvation, apart from works).

Now it is far beyond the scope of this book to dive into these very complex and divisive teachings, so I'm just going to touch on the second one. *Sola fide* was based primarily on texts in Galatians and Romans. Galatians 3, for example, is an entertaining read with sentences such as, "You foolish Galatians! Who has bewitched you?" (Galatians 3:1) and "How can you be so stupid?" (Galatians 3:3). If you read the whole chapter out of context, you will find that Paul is frustrated with the Galatians who seemed to have abandoned his teachings and were once more relying on their works to save them. "It should be obvious that no one is justified in God's sight by the law, for the just man shall live by faith." (Galatians 3:11)

Based on these and other passages, Luther developed a theology that said we could be saved by simply believing in Jesus, and good works were not necessary for salvation. In fact, many people summarize the Gospel message as follows:

- Humans were created in a perfect relationship of love with God.

- Humans sinned and broke that relationship (so we are now damned to Hell).

- Christ died and rose to take away our sin.

- All we need to do is believe and we will be saved.

This basic Gospel message, or kerygma, is summarized so succinctly by John 3:16 that it has become the most popular verse in the Bible: "For God so loved the world that He gave His only Son, that whoever believes in Him may not perish but might have eternal life." (John 3:16)

The thing is, this message is essentially correct, but it is incomplete. When we as Catholics try to point to passages like James 2:24 "A person is justified by works and not by faith alone" or the separation of sheep and goats in Matthew 25:31–46, we are sometimes misunderstood to believe that we can somehow earn our way to Heaven. Even some Catholics are under the impression that that is what we as Catholics believe. The truth is that we are saved by grace, and grace cannot be earned through good works.

However, part of the Gospel message is the transformation wrought by Christ and the Holy Spirit working in us. This transformation is called sanctification, where we are made holy, as God is holy. Our will is conformed to God's will, and we are purified of our sins and attachments. Only in light of this transformation do all kinds of doctrines such as purgatory, Sacraments as the means of grace, and doing acts of penance, make sense. It is also how you can understand Jesus' Sermon on the Mount, where He says things such as, "Be perfect as your heavenly Father is perfect" (Matthew 5:48) and "Not everyone who says "'Lord, Lord' will enter the kingdom but only those who do the will of my Father" (Matthew 7:21). God not only wants to free us from Hell and bring us to Heaven, but He also wants to restore us to our original dignity, in His image and likeness.

How then do we make sense of these passages in Romans and Galatians and the tension between faith and works of the law? Actually, the answer lies right in Galatians. Paul wrote;

> "As for me, brothers, if I am still preaching circumcision, why do the attacks on me continue? If I were, the Cross would be a stumbling block no more. Would that those who are troubling you might go the whole way and castrate themselves!" (Galatians 5:11–12)

Gotta love Paul. He's totally the kind of guy who says something on Facebook, clicks post, and then immediately regrets it—except that he wrote his ideas down and had them read out loud at Christians gatherings all over the known world, and we still quote him two thousand years later.

Paul's concern about the law was about people called Judaizers, who were trying to make all the Christians submit to the laws of the Old Testament. You can imagine the stumbling block that circumcision would present to adult Greek males! They'd come out of baptism and be guided into a back room by a guy with scissors saying, "All right, just one more thing to attend to...."

You can see the early Church wrestling with this theme all throughout Acts and the letters of the Apostles, whether at the council in Jerusalem (Acts 15) or when Peter was instructed to eat unclean animals in a vision (Acts 10) or again when Peter went to visit Cornelius the Gentile (Acts 11). Peter and Paul even argued about it, when Paul confronted Peter for eating with Jews and not Gentiles. (Galatians 2:11–13).

The issue that Paul was concerned about regarding the Galatians was that it appears that they were listening to the Judaizers and thinking that for a Greek to live as a Christian, he must become circumcised and abstain from pork. That is the kind of thing Paul was referring to as "works of the law." He did not mean that Christians needn't concern themselves with moral living.

It should be noted that Catholics sometimes characterize Protestants as thinking that since all that is necessary for salvation is faith in Christ, therefore they needn't obey the moral laws, but this is incorrect. You can't accurately characterize Protestant beliefs at all, since there are so many variations. The vast majority of Protestants believe that faith in Christ is what saves them, but that it necessarily bears the fruit of good works, and so good works are the result of their salvation. The distinction with Catholic teaching in this regard is that Catholics believe being saved is not a one-time thing but is instead an ongoing process resulting from a relationship with Christ and one that includes good works.

Most Christians, whether Catholic or Protestant, agree that to be a disciple means to be in a relationship with God—a relationship that will ultimately be fulfilled in Heaven. Scripture repeatedly compares our relationship with God to a marriage: just as a wife cannot earn a husband through acts of love, so a Christian cannot earn a relationship with God through acts of love. But when a man asks a woman to marry him, he is saying, "Will you let me give myself to you in love, and will you give yourself back to me in love?" So, it is with the covenant God has made with us, and that we in turn have made with God.

While it is correct to say that we cannot earn a relationship with God (salvation) through acts of love, it is also correct to say that we cannot have a relationship with God apart from acts of love. In that sense, there is no salvation without acts of love.

The Law Is Fulfilled in Christ Through Love

Jesus came not to abolish the law, but to fulfill it (Matthew 5:17). In the Old Testament, people obeyed the law out of a legalistic obedience to a master. But Jesus said God is our Father, changing the entire dynamic of how we relate to God, and causing a scandal in the process. In Galatians, Paul again uses the slave and child analogy by comparing us to Hagar and

Sarah in the Old Testament (Galatians 2:21–31): In the Old Covenant, our relationship with God was one of a slave, but in the New Covenant, our relationship is that of a child. A child not only inherits his father's treasure, but he also resembles his father. In the Old Testament, the law was written on slabs of stone, but in the New Testament—the New Covenant—the law is written on our hearts (Jeremiah 31:33; cf. Romans 2:15, Hebrews 8:10). Rather than obeying an external law, we are transformed to be like our Father.

This is why Jesus says that our righteousness must "exceed that of the scribes and the Pharisees" (Matthew 5:20). The scribes were the people who studied and taught about scripture. The Pharisees were the religious elite who insisted that every law be obeyed with extreme precision. Interestingly, these were the people that Jesus had the harshest judgments for. They tithed carefully, they didn't work on the Sabbath, they attended their worship service, and they knew their scriptures. But it was because their righteousness was so outward, without the transformation of the heart, that Jesus criticized them, calling them whitewashed tombs that look clean on the outside but inside are filled with death and rot. (Matthew 23:27–28).

When a woman was caught in adultery, they harshly condemned her and her actions, but Jesus, while still acknowledging that her actions were sinful, was merciful and gentle with her. He loved prostitutes and tax collectors and "sinners" and brought them to repentance.

But to the Pharisees he said, "You snakes! You brood of vipers! How will you escape being condemned to Hell?" (Matthew 23:33) and "You belong to your father, the devil, and you want to carry out your father's desires. He was a murderer from the beginning, not holding to the truth, for there is no truth in him. When he lies, he speaks his native language, for he is a liar and the father of lies" (John 8:44).

I think often we Christians in North America have more in common with the Pharisees then we do with the "sinners." We hear the call to repentance, but instead of recognizing our sin, we say, "Yeah, that call is really important for all of those other people committing sexual sins." We thank God for our own righteousness, but God wants us to come before Him humble, recognizing our own sins (Luke 18:9–14). We can recite the traditional four "sins that cry to Heaven for vengeance"[43] as being murder (Genesis 4:10), sodomy (Genesis 17:20–21), oppression of the poor (Exodus 2:23), and defrauding workers of their just wages (James 5:4), and we say, "Boy, those first two are sure rampant today."

Do we not recognize our own sinfulness? Do we recognize that the second two are also rampant today— and call out to Heaven for vengeance?

I wonder if this is why Pope Francis said, "poverty today is a cry."[44]

---

[43] Henry Tuberville, D.D., *The Douay Catechism of 1649* (New York: P.J. Kennedy, Excelsior Catholic Publishing House, 1833), p.105.

Was Jesus hard on the Pharisees only because they were self-righteous hypocrites? Or also because they were rich and obeyed the law to tithe, but did not care for the poor?

St. Paul wrote, "If I give all I possess to the poor…but do not have love, I am nothing" (1 Corinthians 13:3).

When we examine our conscience in this regard, I think we ask the wrong question. Rather than asking the question, "When I tithe, should I be giving ten percent of my net income or of my gross income?" we should be asking the question, "Do I love my neighbour as myself?"

The missing piece of the Gospel message the way it is sometimes preached is the transformative power of the Holy Spirit. If we are freed from the law of tithing, it is not because we are not going to give, but because our hearts are going to be so transformed that we will actually *want* to give, and to give more. If my heart is changed, the law no longer restricts me because I want to live according to it anyway. Instead of legalistically giving ten percent, we will generously share as much as we can.

Pray for generosity and conversion in your own heart. I said earlier that for years I prayed for detachment daily before I started living according to the values that I thought were true, and of course I need to continue to seek God and let Him transform me more and more,

---

[44] Francis I, "Address to the Students of the Jesuit Schools."

and bring to completion the good work begun in me.

"If we are close to Christ and are following in his footsteps, we will wholeheartedly love poverty, privation, and detachment from earthly things." [45]

The tithe is a great practice, a great place to start. But do not be satisfied with a mere legalistic observance. Let your heart be changed. When God increases your standard of living, let him also increase your standard of giving.

[45] St. Josemaría Escrivá, *The Forge,* 997, retrieved from http://www.escrivaworks.org/book/the_forge-point-997.htm.

Chapter Five Discussion Questions

1. Many Christians continue to tithe even though it is not obligatory. What is your experience with this?

2. Do you struggle to trust God to provide for your material needs?

3. When you impose an exterior discipline on yourself- like a tithe or a luxury budget- does this cause you to become legalistic or does it bring about an interior conversion?

4. Traditionally Catholics teach that there are 4 sins that cry to Heaven for vengeance. Murder, sodomy, oppression of the poor, and defrauding workers of their just wages. Do you think contemporary western society is particularly guilty of these?

Chapter Six
"Woe to You Who Are Rich."
(Luke 6:24)

Perhaps the reason that we have overlooked this teaching, despite the fact that it so often repeated in scripture and Church documents, is because we do not consider ourselves "rich." Of course, we know when we stop to think about it that we *are* rich, and among the richest people in the world. But few of us would describe ourselves as rich, and consequently we gloss over the passages in the Bible addressed to the rich.

My daughter Lucia was prompted to action when my mission trip to Kenya was approaching. She was six years old, and she decided to make sacrifices so that she could give the money to buy shoes for poor kids who don't have any. It really was her own initiative, and she started by looking for cans in ditches that she could recycle and put aside some of her birthday money. She even invited her friends to do likewise, forming a club that she called "The Poorhouse."

She was speaking to one neighbour boy in our mobile home park and explained the purpose of the club, saying, "It's so we rich kids can make sacrifices to give to the poor."

He said, "But I'm not rich."

She said, "Are you kidding me?"

When I speak to young people on this topic, I often start by asking the question, "How many people here would say they are rich?"

Inevitably one or two people at most will put up their hand, and often someone will even say something cute, such as "I'm rich in love because I have such good friends." However, the vast majority of people I encounter do not think of themselves as rich.

I think that we often don't realize just how wealthy we are. I am a youth ministry coordinator—not exactly a high-paying job. I live in a mobile home park and drive a fifteen-year-old minivan. I tend to earn about $20,000 per year less than the average salary for my province in any given year. All of this leaves me with the impression that I am not rich. I'm lower-middle class.

But at the global level, it's different. I was thinking how cool it would be if there was a website which could take into account all kinds of factors, such as income, family size, cost of living, availability of resources like water, electricity, health care, etc., and could generate an algorithm to determine how wealthy an individual was on a bell curve. I have not found anything quite so comprehensive, but I did find a number of websites that will take your salary and determine how wealthy you are on the world scale with a few of the factors considered. The best one I found was www.givingwhatwecan.org.

When I put in my income and then adjusted for taxes and my family size, I discovered that I am in the richest eleven percent of people on the planet. And my income is eleven times the global average. If I recalculate using the average salary in my province, adjusted for average taxes and average family size (two adults and two kids), that family is now in the richest 6.6% of the world's population.

Isn't that astonishing?

Now I'm not going to attempt to consider the many factors that play into our individual wealth and that may skew those results. Let us simply state that the results are staggering, and whatever margin of error there might be does not change the facts: we are phenomenally wealthy. And we are not only rich by world standards today...we are among the wealthiest people in all of history. Never before have people lived in such comfort and luxury.

So, when the Bible says something like, "Woe to you who are rich..." (Luke 6:24), I think we need to sit up and take notice, because the warning is for us.

I had an eye-opening experience on a recent trip to Kenya. Unfortunately, when white people go anywhere in Kenya, there seems to be a hope that since we are wealthy, we may sponsor the organizations that we encounter. I was asked to visit and donate to a health clinic that provides adult circumcision; to sponsor many individuals to go to school; and to provide several people with laptops.

One teenage boy was asking me about life in North America, saying, "I heard that you guys will buy a couch, and then after a year, you'll just throw it in the garbage, and a truck will come get it and will crush it into a tiny block. I also heard that you only keep a car for three years."

Of course, I had to tell him that such stories were exaggerations. However, how strange it must sound to someone in Kenya that people will regularly replace a piece of ten-year-old furniture in North America simply because it's no longer fashionable.

The principal at a school I visited in Nangina seemed also to overestimate my financial means, as she asked me to help pay for the completion of her school building, and she seemed to be of the impression that I would be able to do it myself. The cost would be $50,000 (USD). I found myself embarrassed and tried to tell her that while, yes, I am very wealthy compared to people in Kenya, I simply cannot afford that kind of thing.

She gave us a meal, which consisted of the usual fare including *ugali*, a dish with the consistency of thick oatmeal made from ground and boiled corn, and *chapati*, a kind of flat bread. I was grateful for the meal, and I commented that some of these dishes are not available in Canada. She asked what kind of food we ate in Canada. Again, I was embarrassed as I attempted to explain the concept of a supermarket, with food of all kinds from all over the world, and that in Canada we rarely eat the same supper meal twice in a week.

On another occasion, a woman commented on how she would like to visit Canada, and I told her that if ever she did, she would be welcome to stay with me, although my house was "small and unsuitable" …until I realized that small as my house is, it is bigger than those of anyone I had visited in Kenya.

Maybe it was because I was a preacher, running missions, that I felt especially conflicted. I would spend my days challenging poor people to be holy and to seek God, who I assured them loved them, and then in the evenings I would go to a fancy restaurant for a nice meal while the people who were attending my missions ate a very simple meal of rice and veggies. I didn't stay in the same towns they did because the lodging was unsuitable for someone accustomed to North American living. I needed a bed, and a mosquito net, and clean bottled water, and a flushing toilet. To be honest, I'm not prepared to change those things for future missions. But it felt very strange to finish a talk and be offered a nice cold Coke by one of the locals, and then to drink the Coke in front of kids who never got to enjoy such luxuries…who waited for me to finish so they could have the bottle for deposit.

At any rate, let us simply acknowledge that we are, in fact, rich. I already spent a lot of time establishing the fact that scripture demands that we live generously and self-sacrificially to support the poor. I think it is time to consider specifically some of the passages that address rich people.

We all know the story of Lazarus and the rich man, as told by Jesus. It was a parable about the nature of the afterlife, and usually preachers expound about that theme when they share this story. Maybe we overlook the fact that the rich man appears to have gone to Hell (okay, Hades, but this is where the afterlife question gets really technical), apparently for having done nothing to care for the poor man who lived at his door.

Are we accountable like the rich man was? I suspect most of us, if we had some homeless man sitting at our doorstep, might have fed him, maybe even given him a gift card to McDonalds or a ride to the homeless shelter, and we would hope that he would therefore no longer live on our doorstep. Maybe we even go to the soup kitchen and help serve the poor once a month, and maybe we even give food to the foodbank on a regular basis. I hope we do, and I hope it's enough…but what if it's not?

Our responsibility towards our neighbour extends beyond that of just the people on our doorstep, in our municipality, or even our country. Solidarity must extend to people all over the world. *The Compendium on the Social Doctrine of the Church* attests to this fact: "It is now possible—at least technically—to establish relationships between people who are separated by great distances and are unknown to each other."[46] Because we can help people in Africa, they are our neighbours.

---

[46] *Compendium*, 192.

Jesus made it abundantly clear when He said, "It is harder for a rich man to enter the Kingdom of Heaven than for a camel to pass through the eye of a needle" (Matthew 19:24, Mark 10:25, Luke 18:25). You may have heard people clarify that the "Eye of the Needle" was a very narrow gate in Jerusalem, through which a camel would have to stoop and pass through on its knees, with all its baggage removed. This somewhat softens the message, doesn't it? After all, it's not impossible for a rich person to come into the kingdom, just very difficult, and requiring humility and detachment. Nonetheless, I think it would be wise to regard it as at the very least a caution against wealth.

I was speaking on this scripture verse at a recent "Theology on Tap" event. This event attracts young adult Christians from every denomination, and so when I mentioned the gate to Jerusalem that is called "the eye of the needle," a young Bible college student said, "Oh, I just learned about that yesterday from my professor."

I somewhat awkwardly told him that he should inform his professor that he is wrong and that no such gate exists…and that if his professor asks who told him that, he was to say, "Some Catholic guy at the pub."

Because, as it turns out, no such gate into Jerusalem seems to have existed. Somewhere along the way, this story was invented and repeated, even by such illustrious speakers as me, without the veracity of the story being investigated. The phrase "elephant going through the eye of a needle" is an aphorism used in the Talmud to mean "something impossible."

It is likely that Jesus borrowed from the Talmudic saying when He said it is more difficult for a rich man to enter Heaven than for a camel to pass through the eye of a needle. What He is essentially saying is that it is impossible. Jesus of course qualifies it by saying, "With man this is impossible, but with God all things are possible" (Matthew 19:26).

Christian teachers and apologists seem to feel the need to qualify these hard passages about money: *the eye of the needle was just a narrow gate,* or *money isn't the root of all evil, but the* love *of money is*. Just today I was listening to a Christian radio program that was discussing the Parable of the Rich Fool as found in Luke 12:13–21, wherein a rich man hoards his goods so that he can have a comfortable retirement, and God calls him a fool for not recognizing that he could die tomorrow. The radio program said something like, "Does this mean that God does not want us to have nice things? No. But we should be aware that we could die at any moment and have to give an account of our lives."

I agree with the second half of the program's interpretation, but it does appear to me that the passage is addressing whether or not it is right to hoard wealth for ourselves. It finishes with the line in Luke 12:21: "This is how it will be with whoever stores up things for themselves but is not rich towards God."

Immediately after this Jesus begins the famous passage about the birds and the flowers and not worrying about our material needs. I wonder if maybe Jesus was trying to tell us not to bother saving up for our retirement, but to instead trust in Him?

Stewardship

In Catholic circles, we tend to throw the word "stewardship" around when we talk about our finances. In my experience, we usually say something about how we need to spend our money wisely and invest it so that we aren't wasting it and about how we need to give some amount back to the Church.

But I was thinking about the word "stewardship" recently, and the choice of that word. A steward is someone who takes care of things that do not belong to him. A steward of a castle would manage the castle's affairs for the king while the king is absent. But it's not his own money.

If we are to be good "stewards" of our wealth, this implies that the money does not belong to us, but to God and we will have to make an account of how we spent it.

Consider this in light of Luke 12:32–48. In this passage, Jesus instructs us to sell our possessions and give alms in order to store our treasure in Heaven. He then warns us that we do not know when the Second Coming will be, so we'd better be ready. And He asks the question, "Who then is the faithful and prudent manager who his master will put in charge of the slaves to give them their allowance of food at the proper time?" And He goes on to say, "If that slave says to himself 'My master is delayed in coming,' and he begins to beat the other slaves, men and women, and to eat and drink and get drunk, the master of that slave will come on a day when he does not expect him and at an hour that he does not know, and will cut him in pieces and put him with the unfaithful." This is a very stern warning against being a steward who abuses people and consumes for our own benefit, because we don't know when accounting will be asked of us.

It makes me think of the famous legends of Robin Hood. Robin Hood, as you well know, stole from the rich and gave to the poor. Considering that we must now acknowledge that we are in fact the rich, I wonder how many of us should treat Robin Hood as a hero when we tell our kids the stories?

The villain in the Robin Hood stories is Prince John, who has been given charge of the kingdom of Nottingham while his brother, King Richard the Lionheart, is away, possibly fighting in a crusade. (The story is more legend than history, so a lot of the details get mixed up by the various storytellers, but you get the gist.) At the end of the story, King Richard returns to his rightful throne, dispossessing Prince John for mismanaging his affairs and especially for living in wealth and luxury while the others in the kingdom went hungry. Perhaps like Prince John, our wealth has been entrusted to us as stewards—not so we can live in luxury but so that we can responsibly care for others.

Imagine if you were responsible for many people and their finances and you left someone else in charge for a few years, and upon your return, you found that they had spent your money on themselves while letting others go without. Would you not be outraged at the injustice?

In Canada in recent years, there has been a series of scandals in which senators and other public officials have been misappropriating funds for their own selfish gain. If I spent the money provided to me by my school division to acquire things for myself, I would be fired. If we are stewards, then the money is not ours but God's. If it is God's, we'd better manage it accordingly and be prepared to give an account.

> The rich man—St. Gregory the Great will later say—is only an administrator of what he possesses; giving what is required to the needy is a task that is to be performed with humility because the goods do not belong to the one who distributes them. He who retains riches for himself is not innocent; giving to those in need means paying a debt.[47]

Remember that the foundational principle of the social teaching of the Church is the Universal Destination of Goods. If we want to speak of being good stewards of our finances, this must mean more than just spending our money responsibly so that we can continue to enjoy a high level of consumerism in our retirement years. We are administrators, given the task of meeting the needs of others, and we will be held to account for our stewardship.

I suspect too that this idea of stewardship sheds some light on a very mysterious Bible passage:

> Then Jesus said to the disciples, "There was a

---

[47] *Compendium*, 329.

rich man who had a manager, and charges were brought to him that this man was squandering his property. So, he summoned him and said to him, 'What is this that I hear about you? Give me an account of your management, because you cannot be my manager any longer.' Then the manager said to himself, 'What will I do, now that my master is taking the position away from me? I am not strong enough to dig, and I am ashamed to beg. I have decided what to do so that, when I am dismissed as manager, people may welcome me into their homes.' So, summoning his master's debtors one by one, he asked the first, 'How much do you owe my master?' He answered, 'A hundred jugs of olive oil.' He said to him, 'Take your bill, sit down quickly, and make it fifty.' Then he asked another, 'And how much do you owe?' He replied, 'A hundred containers of wheat.' He said to him, 'Take your bill and make it eighty.' And his master commended the dishonest manager because he had acted shrewdly; for the children of this age are shrewder in dealing with their own generation than are the children of light. And I tell you, make friends for yourselves by means of dishonest wealth so that when it is gone, they may welcome you into the eternal homes." (Luke 16:1–9)

Every time I hear this reading at Mass, I wonder what the priest will say about the fact that it appears that Jesus is commending the guy for being dishonest. Shouldn't the rich man be angry with the manager for ripping him off?

But if the rich man is God, and the manager is us stewards, it sheds a whole new light on the passage: we have been given wealth by God not for our own sake, but so that we can manage it on His behalf. But instead, we squander it on ourselves. Since God is going to demand an accounting for how we spent the money, what should a wise person do?

The answer is given in the parable: forgive debts, and give the money entrusted to them away. If the rich man is God, he won't miss the money. And it suddenly makes sense that He commends the manager for behaving in that way and "welcomes him into eternal homes."

In fact, the phrase translated "dishonest wealth" above is translated "worldly wealth" in other translations. You could also read it as "tainted money." Understanding this passage to mean that God is entrusting a steward with worldly wealth, and that the steward is giving it away to make up for an earlier life of squandering it, also makes way more sense in light of the passages that follow it:

> "Whoever is faithful in a very little is faithful also in much; and whoever is dishonest in a very little is dishonest also in much. If then you have not been faithful with the dishonest (worldly) wealth, who will entrust to you the true riches? And if you have not been faithful with what belongs to another, who will give you what is your own? No slave can serve two masters; for a slave will either hate the one and love the other or be devoted to the one and despise the other. You cannot serve God and

wealth." (Luke 16:10–13)

Whether or not this interpretation is the correct one, it is clear that the principle of stewardship means that the wealth we have is not our own but has been entrusted to us. Rather than squandering it on ourselves, we must use it to build the kingdom of God.

The Life of Luxury

Not only are we wealthy compared to our contemporaries; we are fabulously wealthy compared with anyone in history. An interesting study can be done on the history of the term "luxury" itself. The word entered the lexicon around AD 1300, and at that time it meant "lasciviousness" or "sinful self-indulgence." The terms in Old French and Latin clearly indicate excess and extravagance. It remained a pejorative term right up to the seventeenth century.

But today we don't only live in luxury—we celebrate it! When someone shows us their beautiful new house or car or home renovation, we congratulate them, encouraging them to do more of the same. We watch those commercials with taglines like "you deserve it," and we just buy the pitch. Someone tells us about the great expensive vacation they are going on, and we say things like, "Good for you! I'm glad to see you treating yourself well" when in fact these values are directly opposed to the Christian values of self-sacrifice and love. We have so bought into our world's culture that we don't even notice the contradiction.

We wouldn't do this with other forms of sin. If a man is

looking at pornography, we don't celebrate with him his excellent taste in women. While throughout history Christians have celebrated and canonized those who lived simple lives of generosity, today we Christians discuss the universal call to holiness while attending retreats in luxurious hotels or retreat centres. We even have things like luxury Christian cruises. To those who went before us who saw the word "luxury" as implicitly sinful, I wonder if this wouldn't sound as ridiculous as "lascivious Christian cruises" or "hedonistic Christian cruises."

Hedonism

When we think of hedonism, we probably think of the pursuit of unrestrained sensual pleasure, a worldview which is directly contrary to the worldview of Christians. However, I want to suggest that this is precisely the worldview that we, alongside our non-Christian contemporaries, are allowing to inform the majority of our decisions.

As Christians, we show some sexual restraint—or at least we firmly resolve to do so. And we are not as inclined to drunkenness as we might otherwise be. But are we any less materialistic or gluttonous than everyone else? If hedonism is the worldview that says the highest aim and purpose of human life is to seek pleasure, is this so different from the typical Christian's lifestyle that has enshrined the pursuit of happiness?

You might think I'm going too far on this point, but I think it deserves some consideration. For Christians, the purpose of life is to love— ultimately to love God, but also to love others: "For whoever does not love a brother or sister whom they have seen, cannot love God whom they have not seen" (1 John 4:20). But when we think about our finances and make plans, how much time and resources do we put towards loving others and how much serves our own selfishness?

We make certain to put enough away for a comfortable retirement so that we can continue to enjoy the life we have grown accustomed to. Is comfort for an older person the equivalent of pleasure for a younger person? Old people don't want the rush and excitement typically associated with the term "hedonism," so for them you might expect that living for pleasure would look different.

When we choose to spend our resources and time on entertainment and fine dining and comfortable homes—as we all do—are we at that moment seeking to love, in keeping with our stated life philosophy, or are we just seeking personal enjoyment?

I think this underlying philosophy—that the purpose of life is happiness—is so ingrained and unquestioned in our culture that this is why people have so much difficulty understanding Christian teachings…and why we as Christians have so much difficulty explaining it.

If something bad happens to someone, we say, "Well, God works all things to the good of those who love Him" (Romans 8:28); this is true, but we assume that the "good" mentioned here is the greater happiness of the individual, when God's purpose for us, the "good in God's eye," is greater love.

Therefore when people ask, "why do bad things happen to good people?" and we struggle to find the "good" thing that comes out of the bad, it may be because we define the word 'good' incorrectly. The reason our culture so rejects the logic of our sexual ethic is because it has assumed the logic of hedonism, where the only ethical restriction remaining is "pursue happiness but do not infringe on the happiness of others." Who can make sense out of the prohibition against contraception within that framework? And why would anyone work on a difficult and failing marriage if the end goal of life is personal happiness?

It is largely for this reason that our sexual ethic does not make sense and has been rejected by our culture; even we have forgotten the logical root of it, and so we live according to superficial sets of rules. As with tithing, an obedient Catholic will obey the rule about contraception, but it is the transformation of the heart that is desired.

Is it any wonder then that St. Paul wrote, "Love of money is the root of every kind of evil?" (1 Timothy 6:10). In capitalist countries, a philosophy of consumption was deliberately fostered because it would drive the economy. Christians have bought into that philosophy wholeheartedly, despite the fact that at its roots are decidedly unchristian ideas.

There is a fascinating discussion taking place in the United States about how that country's Christians came to identify so fully with the political right. I recommend the book *One*

Nation under God; How Corporate America invented Christian America by Kevin M Kruse. Kruse details how corporate interests and Christian interests aligned in reaction to the New Deal and later to the Communist Menace. Such influential men as Dwight D. Eisenhower, Billy Graham and Walt Disney all had a hand in forming America's identity as a Christian nation, in a time when the words "Under God" were added to the pledge of allegiance and the motto "In God we trust" to the currency.

What I find most interesting for our purposes is how evangelical and other Christian leaders took up the arguments that communism is inherently opposed to Christianity because it denies our dignity and freedoms under God and puts the state in the place of God. While this may be true, have we in reaction to it fostered the idea that unbridled capitalism and Christianity are synonymous?

It appears that this has happened to such a great extent that when Pope Francis reinforces the Church's teachings that seek to limit capitalism, the pope's message is viewed as anti-American—and even anti-Christian!—by some.

The Christian message is not about overthrowing capitalism, but about conversion of hearts. Have our hearts bought in to the entire capitalist worldview so much that we no longer recognize the Christian imperative to love?

I would like to emphatically repeat this point: I am not arguing 'for' communism or 'against' capitalism. Rather, I am arguing for love and against greed. It is a change of heart that is needed. I suspect that many people fail to distinguish between moral values and political values. In fact, communism is antithetical to Christianity in part because it does not allow for true generosity. When people are compelled by the state to virtue, it is not virtue at all. We must willingly and freely embrace the values of Christ.

Salt of the Earth

By in large, Christians in North America do not appear to be living differently from our contemporaries. Our houses are just as nice. Our cars, our vacations, our standards of living are all just as luxurious as those of our non-Christian neighbours. Jesus said, "You are the salt of the earth. But if salt loses its saltiness, how can it be made salty again? It is no longer good for anything, except to be thrown out and trampled underfoot" (Matthew 5:13).

If we are going to be the salt of the earth, we must be different from everyone else.

Within the same sermon, Jesus also compares us to a city on a hill and to a light that should not be put under a bushel. This theme is popular fodder for Christian art and music, and Christians will gleefully sing about how we are the light of the world and how Jesus is shining through us. But what is it that ought to be different about us that people will see as a light?

Jesus actually tells us: "In the same way, let your light shine before others, that they may see your good deeds and glorify your Father in Heaven" (Matthew 5:16).

How can we be a light when our values and deeds are the same as everybody else's? In regard to money, we have conformed to our age. Jesus said, "By this everyone will know that you are my disciples, if you love one another" (John 13:35). No wonder our efforts to evangelize are failing. In fact, in rich countries, the faith is on the decline. If we are not salt and light, we are useless.

Imagine on the other hand how much more effective we would be if we adopted these values of simplicity as outlined in scripture. Pope Francis said, "Practicing charity is the best way to evangelize."[48]

St. Francis of Assisi is popularly believed to have said, "Preach the Gospel always; when necessary, use words." I once organized a whole retreat to young adults that focused on evangelization, and among them were trained evangelists with Catholic Christian Outreach (CCO), which is described as "a Catholic university movement that seeks to form intentional disciples who know and practice the Church's mandate to evangelize." I presented one of the talks entitled "Preach the Gospel Always; When Necessary, Use Words" because I knew that using that title would make the CCO staffers nervous. For one thing, many people have used this message as an excuse to not actually preach the Gospel and evangelize. I also knew that St. Francis never even said it.

But he did say something like it: "No friar may preach contrary to Church law or without the permission of the

---

[48] Francis I, Twitter post (January 24, 2015), retrieved from https://twitter.com/pontifex/status/558918164604399617?lang=en.

minister. The minister, for his part, must be careful not to grant permission indiscriminately. All the friars, however, should preach by their example."[49]

So far from giving us an out from evangelizing, Francis preached everywhere he went and used words when he did so, and he trained others to do so as well. However, supposing he had said it: how would we go about preaching the Gospel without using words?

Is your life so remarkably loving that your co-workers and colleagues are coming to accept the Gospel based solely on your example?

I would suggest that the life of Mother Teresa was that loving. And so was the life of St. Francis. If we are all called to be saints, to be truly holy, each uniquely transformed into the likeness of God, then I suspect that people would see our love, and it would be the evidence of the truth of Christianity, and we would not need to use words. But at this moment, words are desperately needed.

A few years ago, I watched a debate between Tony Blair and Christopher Hitchens. The question being debated was, "Is religion a force for good in the world?" Now the question was flawed for several reasons. First, it had Blair defending outrageous things done in the name of Islam and other religions, even though he is a Christian. Second, to debate the question presupposes that no particular religion is correct. You can't very well argue in this context that

---

[49] St. Francis of Assisi, *First Rule* (1221), s.17.

"Christianity is a force for good because in it people find the truth and forgiveness for their sins and an eternal relationship with God." Even though those are the claims Christianity makes, you can't objectively prove those claims without first proving Christianity. If Christianity is true, then it is good for the world because it teaches us what is true. But again, Blair could not speak of the truth of religion because he had to defend mutually exclusive religions like Hinduism and Christianity at the same time.

Instead, Blair was made to find things that everyone agreed was good that religion brought to the world, while Hitchens could point to things that everyone believed was bad. Besides the fact that Hitchens was probably the more skilled debater, and that by their own admission 55% of the audience already agreed with his position (giving him a sort of home field advantage), Hitchens also had a much easier time of it since he had only to point to the sensationalistic horrors done in the name of any religion to establish that "religion" was a force for evil in the world.

But the question itself is interesting. Supposing that instead the question had been, "Is Mother Teresa a force for good in the world"? I suspect that while Hitchens actually did question her sanctity, he would have a much harder time demonstrating that she was not a force for good. This is because Mother Teresa became the saint that God called her to be, whereas I think many of us Christians have a form of godliness but have denied the power of our faith (cf. 2 Timothy 3:5).

The work of God in us is to make us holy, but we continue

to turn to our idols, and specifically to money despite the warning from Christ that "you cannot serve God and money." (Matthew 6:24, Luke 16:13). The power of God is hindered in us because, as Jesus said, our souls are thorny ground where the seed of the Word falls and the thorns choke the plant: "The seed falling among the thorns refers to someone who hears the word, but the worries of this life and the deceitfulness of wealth choke the word, making it unfruitful" (Matthew 13:22).

How much more credible would our faith be in the world if the lives we lived were consistent with what our church teaches regarding money? In the debate, Tony Blair did make the point that Christians do incredible charitable work around the world—a point that Hitchens seemed to think was discredited due to the fact that it was so obvious. It is often said that the Catholic Church is the largest charitable organization on the planet, a claim made, for example, in the commercials by Catholics Come Home on television. I was unable to verify that claim; however, it is certainly difficult to imagine what other organization might be contesting for the title.

There is much to celebrate, but there is still much to do.

Why Do Educated Countries Reject Christianity?

Another argument frequently heard against Catholicism is that if Christianity is true, then why is it that as countries become more educated, more people reject the faith? Of course, we can debate this head-on and talk about intellectual pride and how the Cross of Christ is foolishness to those who are perishing and how Christ selects those who are foolish in the eyes of the world (cf. 1 Corinthians 1:27), but the correlation is not necessarily indicative of causation.

It does appear to be true that the more educated countries have a higher level of rejection of Christianity. However, it is also the case that the more educated countries are also the richer countries—the ones that serve money more. When Jesus said, "You cannot serve God and money" and that the "deceitfulness of wealth will choke the word," was He just speaking in hyperbole, or is He describing a spiritual truth? Look again at what He says: "No one can serve two masters. Either you will hate the one and love the other, or you will be devoted to the one and despise the other. You cannot serve both God and money" (Matthew 6:24).

Hold the phone! You will be devoted to one and despise the other? I know plenty of people who are devoted to money and despise God, but do you know any who are devoted to God but despise money?

Does wealth actually threaten our faith? Consider Ireland. It has been said that what eight hundred years of occupation and three hundred years of religious persecution failed to do, a mere thirty years of prosperity has succeeded in bringing about. Something similar can be said about some of the Eastern Bloc states: that what eighty years of communist ideology failed to do, twenty years of capitalism succeeded.

St. Josemaría Escrivá warned us about the dangers of being overly attached to things;

Detach yourself from people and things until you are stripped of them. For, says Pope Saint Gregory, the devil has nothing of his own in this world, and naked he comes to battle. If you go clothed to fight him, you will soon be pulled to the ground: for he will have something to catch you by.[50]

St. Paul said that our love of money amounts to idolatry (cf. Colossians 3:5 and Ephesians 5:5). Why is a love of money so incompatible with allowing the Word to bear fruit in our lives? Pope Francis put it this way: "Almost without being aware of it, we end up being incapable of feeling compassion at the outcry of the poor, weeping for other people's pain, and feeling a need to help them, as though all this were someone else's responsibility and not our own. The culture of prosperity deadens us; we are thrilled if the market offers us something new to purchase; and in the meantime, all those lives stunted for lack of opportunity seem a mere spectacle; they fail to move us."[51]

If Jesus was correct when He said, "You cannot serve God and money", then you would expect that as nations increasingly serve money, they would stop serving God.

Happy Are the Poor

When we Christians buy into the hedonistic and greedy assumptions of the culture around us, it does indeed make us

---

[50] St. Josemaría Escrivá, *The Way*, 149, retrieved from http://www.escrivaworks.org/book/the_way-point-149.htm.

[51] Francis I, *Evangelii Gaudium*, s.54.

"incapable of feeling compassion at the outcry of the poor."[52] I have personally encountered this both in myself and in the objections raised to this message: "The poor have no electricity or indoor plumbing. Neither did our grandparents. Big deal!" Or very often, I have heard people say about their encounters with poor people that "they have so little, but they are so happy."

I just have to say that this was not my impression, at least not entirely. I did meet some extremely happy poor people, who had a right Christian attitude towards money and were detached from it and from ambition and so were thankful for what little they had. One of the most beautiful things on a mission trip is when you have an opportunity to serve in a poor, rural parish, where the people are happy, the music is great, and the worship is authentic. But I also met large numbers of people who found their economic situation very difficult and stressful.

We are currently living through a massive migration phenomenon, which shows no signs of stopping. Refugees from conflicts and poverty are overwhelming Europe and impacting every nation in the world. It seems that almost monthly, Americans are finding new tactics to stop the flow of illegal migrants along their southern border.

Recently I was watching *The Fiddler on the Roof* with my kids. Spoiler alert! At the end of the movie, all the Jews are evicted from Anatevka, the town in Russia where their families had lived for generations. My children found it

---

[52] Francis I, *Evangelii Gaudium*, s.54.

quite distressing and were asking for explanations, so I likened it to the situation in Syria and the refugees whom we had helped welcome into Rocky Mountain House, and who my children know by name.

My daughter, Lucia, said, "Yes, but that's only one family! We need to help more!"

I told her that the only way to help more families was to make more sacrifices. It is strange to come to a point, and to see your children come to a point, where rather than wanting money so we can acquire more for ourselves, we really wish we had more money so we can help others.

But as everyone knows, while Syrians are the biggest newsmakers, the migrants flooding Europe are not all Syrians, nor are they all refugees, and this has become one of the major sticking points in the debate about what to do with them. Many of them are economic migrants, taking advantage of the unstable global situation so they can get to Germany or the United Kingdom or somewhere where there is a promise of a better life.

The question I want to ask is if they are in fact "economic migrants," is this why are they migrating? If the narrative that poor people are truly happy was accurate, why would they sacrifice so much and risk so much to come to our countries? Because it's not just Middle Eastern people and Africans running to Europe; it's also Asians running to Australia and Latin Americans flooding into the United States. They are leaving their families and homes behind to come to a country where they are foreigners (often illegal immigrants) and unable to find suitable work. They don't speak the language, they are discriminated against, and in order to come here, they risk all kinds of hazards to their lives, including being taken advantage of, both financially and sexually, all so they can live as second-class non-citizens in our countries?

These are not choices "happy" people would make.

I have a friend named Joy who lives in my town in Canada. She is from the Philippines, and she migrated here so that she could live in a small apartment with three other Filipinos and work at Harvey's. The income she makes at her minimum-wage fast food job helps her to support her four children whom she left behind in order to work here. Stories like hers can be told all over wealthy western nations. Somehow leaving your children to work at a fast-food restaurant and live in an overcrowded apartment in a cold country is preferable to the situation they left behind.

When I first went to Kenya, I was teaching about the Theology of the Body to a group of young people. It took me a while to realize that in a country where very few people had a university education, perhaps the subjects I was teaching on went unnecessarily deep.

I finished what I thought was a strong presentation summarizing Pope John Paul II's essential teachings and asked if there were any questions. A high school girl raised her hand and asked, "So is it okay to have sex on the first date?"

Apparently, I had failed to address some key points.

After the presentation a young man came up to me and asked if he could speak to me more privately. I agreed and walked with him out of the compound and to his home. The compound where we were staying included a church, a hospital, and other facilities run by the Church, and was surrounded by a stone wall with barbed wire on top. The gate was guarded by an armed guard, and before Sunday Mass, everyone attending had to go through a metal detector for protection. Until this moment, I had not had the courage to wander far from the compound.

The young man's name was Steve, and he walked with me to his house. Unfortunately, this was one of those times when I wished I had a camera but was too ashamed to carry mine, because it was too blatant a symbol of my affluence.

Steve's house was small—I'd estimate about ten feet by eight feet. Or, put another way, smaller than my child's bedroom in my mobile home. He shared it with his three adult brothers. A small bunk bed stood along one wall and served as the bed for all four adult men. On the floor was the metal cylinder charcoal stove, and on another wall was a table with a small pile of clothes that the brothers shared. When I asked where they went to the bathroom, he pointed towards a field full of garbage, which could be accessed by walking to the end of the row of conjoined houses.

"You go right out in the open?" I asked.

"It's even worse for the women," he told me. "They are

often too ashamed or scared to go during the day, so they hold it all day and wait until after dark."

I need not tell you what risks the women were taking by going in the dark.

Steve's question was this, "There is a rich woman who pays me to have sex with her. What should I do?"

Relying on my homegrown Catholic youth minister wisdom, I said simply, "Well it's a sin, so despite the hardship you will face, you should repent and tell her you can't see her anymore."

"But she is paying for my housing." he protested. Like many North Americans, I was not aware that people living in slums are paying rent for the privilege of doing so.

"I'm sorry, but you still have to turn away from sin."

"But she will pay for my university. Whatever future I have depends on her."

"Wow, that's tough. But you know, we need to trust in the goodness of God…"

"If I leave her…she is rich. She will hire men to come after me and threaten me."

"Can you go to the police?"

"No! She's rich!" he said emphatically, as if I should pick up the obvious implications of that statement. "If I go to the police, she will bribe them and make an accusation against me, and I myself will go to prison!"

I later asked a local who does prison ministry in Kenya, and he confirmed that this was likely the case.

More recently I visited another home which was even worse. I was in Mexico City with Renewal Ministries. We were providing food, clothing, and medicine for the people who lived and worked in the dumps. These people make their living by sorting through the garbage and finding recyclables that they can sell. Many of them have built their homes in the dump itself out of whatever they can find, pallets and tarps and wires and scraps of wood.

On our second day there, a man named Daniel offered to show me his home. So, I left the area where we had set up a clinic and walked with him into the slum.

His home was very small, with tarps for walls and a dirt floor, and featured some junk: an old dirty stuffed dog, a makeshift shrine to "Holy Death." I think the area of the room was about the size of a queen-sized mattress. He'd sleep on the dirt floor, along with his wife Nancy, and his four children, Daniela, Diana, Donatillo, and Darian. I mention their names because I regard them as my friends.

You see, the difficulty is that these people are not living "like my grandparents did." They are not simply lacking in electricity and plumbing. The whole system is broken there. Security is a major issue. Justice is an issue. Healthcare is an issue. Corruption in politics is an issue.

I had an opportunity to visit a few prisons on my trip. The

men's prison reminded me of a prisoner of war camp from movies like *The Great Escape*. The men wore striped pajamas, slept in large dorms with several beds (I did not see the inside of the buildings), and lived in compounds surrounded by barbed wire.

The women's prison bothered me even more. I don't know what the women did, or what they were accused of, but it angered me when the guards prodded them into their crowded dorms with their batons. Some would say my sympathies are misplaced, but as a Christian I remember Christ's question, "when I was in prison, did you visit me?" (cf. Matthew 25:36).

The women also wore shapeless striped pajamas, which were humiliating, I thought, in how unflattering they were. I don't know if makeup or hair accessories would be permitted, but they might give the women a little dignity. As it was, we brought the women soap and toilet paper, as otherwise these are luxuries the state would not have provided for them. I felt like a fool grinning for a photo while handing over these essential supplies to prisoners who received them on behalf of the other inmates, as if I were handing over an oversized cheque.

There were children in the women's prison, and my understanding is that if a woman with a young child was arrested, her child would go with her until the child was five years old. It was unclear to me what happened to the child at that point, but I was led to believe that they would have to leave the prison. I hope that they are given to someone who can care for them.

When I went to leave the prison, an inmate suddenly ran over to me and handed me a letter. Caught off-guard, I was insufficiently discreet with it, and so the warden noticed it and demanded that she have the opportunity to read it. "Please," the inmate pled. "I just want him to read it!" But the warden was adamant, so the inmate took back her letter, and I never discovered its contents. I was told that in all likelihood, it was a plea for money. Many of the inmates might actually be innocent, but they are waiting for their court dates. However, in order to secure a court date, they have to pay for the legal services. Unable to pay, they languish in prison until some family member or friend brings them the funding.

Because the whole country is poor, basic services, such as care for those in prison, are simply not available. I met a doctor from the United States who told me that in the hospital he was working in Kenya, they would often have three patients in a bed. I'm not comfortable sharing a bed with a stranger in the first place, much less two who may have infectious diseases.

He told me that the hospital had armed guards at the gate. I was not surprised by this, since this precaution was also necessary at churches, schools, and hotels. However, in the case of the hospital, the guards' duties were more for keeping people in the hospital than for keeping them out. If people came in for treatment but were unable to pay, they were prevented from leaving until the money was acquired—this, in an already overcrowded hospital!

We do not realize just how many hardships the poor face in these countries until we consider all of these factors. Consider your own family for a moment and imagine what it would be like if you were in one of these countries and unable to afford healthcare.

In my family, neither I nor my mom would have survived my birth. But let us assume that I had, and that my wife hadn't died during her first labour either, which she almost certainly would have. Because of the various ailments we have, I would by now be blind, my wife would have died, and my daughter would be crippled and in pain, with quickly deteriorating eyes. And even this scenario assumes that we would only have the diseases we developed in Canada, with no additional problems from malaria or other diseases associated with unhygienic conditions,

I believe that our love for the poor, which is supposed to be characteristic of Catholics, should prompt us to want to do something for them, to help ease their suffering in this world. "Suppose a brother or a sister is without clothes and daily food. One of you says to them, "Go in peace; keep warm and well fed" but does nothing about their physical needs, what good is it? In the same way, faith by itself, if it is not accompanied by action, is dead" (James 2:15–17).

There is a demand of justice on us, the rich, to care for the poor and to meet their daily needs. But beyond justice, we must respond to them in love. Wealth can become an idol, and as Christians we must be so notably different from our contemporaries that people who see us will say, "See how they love each other?" When we conform to the materialistic culture that surrounds us, we run the very real risk of losing our faith, our souls, and our love for the poor.

Chapter Six Discussion Questions

1. Do you think of yourself as rich?

2. Peter proposed that you try comparing your wealth to global standards at givingwhatwecan.org. If you haven't tried it, take a moment now and then discuss.

3. Jesus taught us that it is harder for a rich man to get into heaven than for a camel to pass through the eye of a needle. (Cf. Matthew 19:24) Have you heard the qualification before that the eye of the needle was a gate into Jerusalem? In so far as there was no such gate, how should we interpret this passage?

4. Have you noticed that when Christian speakers address passages on money, like the eye of the needle (Mt. 19:24), love of money is the root of all evil (1 Tim 6:10) and you cannot serve God and money (Mt. 6:24), they frequently qualify them to downplay the challenging message they seem to be clearly communicating? In light of the consistent message of scripture and church teaching, do you think these qualifications are accurate? Why are so many Christian leaders quick to dismiss the hard teaching on money?

5. We are to be stewards of our goods, because they are not ours but Gods. Does being a good steward mean only maintaining what was given

to us, or does it also mean distributing wealth? When you enjoy luxuries, do you feel entitled to them?

6. Do you affirm people when they make choices to live in luxury, such as purchase an unnecessarily nice home or vehicle or vacation? Are things like luxury cruises and vacations justifiable in light of the Universal Destination of Goods?

7. Peter suggests that for the world the purpose of life is comfort and happiness, while for Christians it is love. How ought this distinction change the way we live our lives as Christians compared to our contemporaries? How does it affect the way we struggle with theological questions, such as why does God allow suffering?

8. How do you think Christians in the west came to identify so strongly with capitalist ideals?

9. As salt and light, the Christian life should be so different from the rest of society that people would be drawn to Christ through our witness. Do you think that if Christians joyfully embraced simplicity it would lend credibility to the faith? Does our mediocre response to this challenge undermine the authenticity of our message?

10. Peter suggests that the reason people in educated countries are rejecting the faith is not actually caused by the education of the populace, but by the wealth. Discuss.

11. People often talk about meeting poor people in developing countries and describe the joy they see there. Peter says that he has witnessed that phenomenon himself; however, he points out that poor people consistently risk their lives to immigrate to rich countries, something they would not do if they were happy. Do you think the extremely poor are on the whole happier or less happy than the rich?

12. Does emphasizing the 'happiness of the poor' contribute to making us, in the words of Pope Francis, "incapable of feeling compassion at the outcry of the poor"?

13. It is easy to imagine, even as outsiders, how complicated life gets when the whole society is poor. Discuss different ways that systems like infrastructure, policing, medicine, etc, would be affected by not having a strong tax base.

Chapter Seven
Transformed by Love

"If I give all I possess to the poor…but do not have love, I gain nothing" (1 Corinthians 13:3).

Recently on Facebook I posted that I wish people who follow my philosophy had a particular title by which to identify themselves, so that others would immediately understand my values from the title—similar to how if someone identifies as a vegetarian, you can typically assume that they won't eat a burger because of a value of kindness to animals. The whole thing was just a set-up, with the punchline being that people who practice simplicity should just identify as simpletons.

But Facebook being what it is, my friends responded with all kinds of suggestions from frugaloid to simplifitarian to minimalist. I don't know what a frugaloid or a simplifitarian is, but I know what a minimalist is. The thing about minimalists is they try to live with only one hundred possessions for the sake of living with one hundred possessions. They may have a really great television and no DVDs because they have Netflix and other digital "possessions" that don't count. But the Church's philosophy of simplicity is not simplicity for its own sake, but for the sake of love.

St. Josemaría Escrivá wrote about how as Christians we place much value on virtues such as temperance and humility, and yet Christ did not say "you will be known as my chosen ones because you are not gluttons or drunkards"[53] or "you will be known as my disciples by your modesty and humility."[54]

I might also add that Jesus did not say we would be recognized as disciples by the creed we profess, by our voting patterns, or by our choice to only listen to radio stations that are safe and fun for the whole family. Of course, what Jesus did say was, "by this everyone will know that you are my disciples, if you love one another" (John 13:35).

To be a Christian means to be anointed by the Holy Spirit to continue the work of Christ in the world. This includes His redemptive work, because part of what it means to be "saved" or "born again" is to be restored to the likeness of God. This process of transformation is called "purgation" in the West or "deification" in eastern Catholic Churches. As the priest says in the liturgy of the Eucharist, "we come to share in the divinity of Christ who humbled Himself to share in our humanity."

While I endorse the concept of a luxury budget as an exterior discipline, because remember that exterior discipline leads to interior conversion. Otherwise, the luxury budget itself can become, like the tithe, merely an external legalism. As we are sanctified and made "perfect as our heavenly Father is perfect" (Matthew

---

[53] Josemaría Escrivá, *Friends of God*, 43, retrieved from http://www.escrivaworks.org/book/friends_of_god-point-43.htm.

[54] Josemaría Escrivá, *Friends of God*, 44, retrieved from http://www.escrivaworks.org/book/friends_of_god-point-44.htm.

5:48), we will see the vices in ourselves, such as greed and covetousness and anxiety, being replaced by virtues such as gratitude and generosity and detachment.

In this chapter, we will examine some practical things we can do to overcome our greedy natures, with the help of God's grace.

Do Not Covet

> "You shall not covet your neighbour's house;
> you shall not covet your neighbour's wife,
> or his male servant, or his female servant,
> or his ox, or his donkey,or anything
> that is your neighbour's."
> ~Exodus 20:17~

I was playing Scrabble online one day (clearly a pastime for those already perfected by grace) when suddenly an ad popped up for another smartphone app called "Covet Fashion." Now I didn't play the game (clearly, I am not the target audience), but curiosity did drive me to check it out on the internet. It appears that the purpose of the game is to create an avatar (a "digital character") who then tries on the latest real-world fashions. The idea is obvious from the name of the game: covet. It is a clever marketing gimmick that creates the desire for real-world products.

It's the name that gets me. Covet. Where did I hear that word again? Oh yeah, in the Ten Commandments. There's a commandment that actually begins, "Thou shalt not covet..." In fact, there are two commandments that start that way according to the Catholic divisions.[55]

Doesn't that seem like a weird commandment, though? Like, do you think God just really wanted to round it off with an even ten, so he threw two coveting ones in? I mean, most of the commandments are honoured in modern law (don't steal, don't murder, don't bear false witness (perjury), etc.), but who cares if you wish you had a donkey as nice as your neighbour's?

Catholics love to create examinations of conscience based on the Ten Commandments, with a list of possible ways that we offended against them after each commandment heading. But arriving at Commandments Nine and Ten, we find they are often either clumped together and have two subcategories, or they are lumped in with "don't steal" and "don't commit adultery," since really they just repeat those precepts.

But the Church has consistently held that not only is covetousness a sin, but it is one of the seven deadly sins. In case you go and look it up, it is also called "greed" in many lists. "Put to death, therefore, whatever belongs to your earthly nature: sexual immorality, impurity, lust, evil desires, and greed, which is idolatry" (Colossians 3:5).

---

[55] The Ten Commandments are not numbered in scripture, but they are described as being ten in number, so Catholics and Protestants have numbered the Commandments differently from one another.

Covetousness or greed is a deadly sin that we should put to death, "for on account of these things the wrath of God is coming" (Colossians 3:6). St. Thomas Aquinas addressed covetousness in his *Summa Theologiae*:

> "Hence it must needs be that man's good in their respect consists in a certain measure, in other words, that man seeks, according to a certain measure, to have external riches, in so far as they are necessary for him to live in keeping with his condition of life. Wherefore it will be a sin for him to exceed this measure, by wishing to acquire or keep them immoderately. This is what is meant by covetousness, which is defined as "immoderate love of possessing." It is therefore evident that covetousness is a sin."[56]

Our entire culture has been built on the principles of consumerism. This was done deliberately, as consumerism creates wealth for the entire nation. This consumerism is a philosophy that is directly opposed to Christianity, is unsustainable and leading to destruction even by non-Christian standards and has become a form of idolatry which is incompatible with the love of and service to God.

---

[56] Thomas Aquinas, *Summa Theologiae,* II-II, Q. 118, Art. 1, translated by the Fathers of the English Dominican Province

Consumerism is driven in large part by advertising. The game "Covet Fashion" tells you point-blank what its intentions are, but almost all advertising is the same. Advertising is essentially an attempt to try to make you covet a product that likely exceeds the measure of what you need.

The problem is that we subject ourselves to this endorsement of sin all day, and we don't even notice. I think that one of the challenges of living simply in alignment with the Gospel is that we keep seeing advertising on television or the internet or whatever other media we consume, and this marketing is directly opposed to our efforts to become detached from the things of this world. How can we "put to death" the "greed which is idolatry" if every time we relax, we consume something that increases in us our greed? Every Christian knows that if we want to fight lust, a good first step is to avoid watching porn. But I suspect that the reason we've bought into this culture of consumerism so wholeheartedly is because we continue to allow that culture to influence our hearts and minds.

So practically speaking, I suggest that if you want to reduce your materialism, stop consuming advertising. Don't watch commercials—or maybe don't even watch television. Don't flip through catalogues, go shopping as a pastime, or try to keep up with the latest fashions or technology.

It reminds me of that old Cherokee parable of the two wolves at war within us: one wolf represents all that is evil—anger, jealousy, greed, guilt, resentment—while the other wolf represents all that is good—joy, peace, love, hope. Which one wins the battle for your heart? The one that you feed. If you really want to put to death the greed within you, stop feeding it!

I also suggest that we recognize how much our culture praises consumerism. Don't we all admire and flatter our friends when they renovate their homes, buy a hot new car, or wear an expensive new outfit? Don't we even feel obligated to do so? Of course, it is nice to celebrate with our friends their accomplishments and the good things that befall them, but by praising one another for our material wealth, we are just reinforcing the values of consumerism.

Every time I feel like I'm being too extreme, I find another quote in the Bible or by a saint that goes even further. The following excerpt is from Church Father of Alexandria in his second-century sermon, "Who Is the Rich Man That Shall Be Saved?"

> "Those who bestow laudatory addresses on the rich appear to me to be rightly judged not only flatterers and base, in vehemently pretending that things which are disagreeable give them pleasure, but also godless and treacherous; godless, because neglecting to praise and glorify God, who is alone perfect and good, of whom are all things, and by whom are all things, and for whom are all things (Romans 11:36), they invest with divine honours men wallowing in an execrable

and abominable life, and, what is the
principal thing, liable on this account to
the judgment of God; and treacherous,
because, although wealth is of itself
sufficient to puff up and corrupt the souls
of its possessors, and to turn them from
the path by which salvation is to be
attained, they stupefy them still more, by
inflating the minds of the rich with the
pleasures of extravagant praises, and by
making them utterly despise all things
except wealth, on account of which they
are admired; bringing, as the saying is,
fire to fire, pouring pride on pride, and
adding conceit to wealth, a heavier
burden to that which by nature is a
weight, from which somewhat ought
rather to be removed and taken away as
being a dangerous and deadly disease."[57]

Often when I talk about the fact that living in luxury
while others go hungry is sin and contrary to charity, I
hear the argument that St. Paul said that "the love of
money" is the root of all evil, not money itself—as
though that somehow nullifies the point. But it's true; it
is love of money that is the root of evil, greed that is
idolatry, covetousness that Thomas Aquinas describes
as a "capital vice which gives rise to other vices,"[58] and

---

[57] Clement of Alexandra, "Who Is the Rich Man That Shall Be Saved?",
s.1.

[58] Thomas Aquinas, *Summa Theologiae*, II-II, Q. 118, Art. 7, translated by

the service of money that Jesus says is incompatible with service to God. In the end, this is in actual fact an even higher calling than that to live in outward simplicity. I can almost imagine Jesus saying, "You've heard it said, 'Do not live in luxury while others are in need,' but I tell you should not even desire these luxuries that might impede your salvation."

If we are going to weaken and kill the wolf called avarice, the first thing we should do is cut off its food supply.

Virtue and Vice

> "Watch out! Be on your guard against all kinds
> of greed; life does not consist in an
> abundance of possessions."
> ~Luke 12:15~

So how do we do that? How do we defeat the wolf of vice? Partly by starving it, and partly by feeding the wolf of virtue instead.

There is an age-old wisdom in the Church that if you want to fight a vice, the best way of defeating it is by developing the opposite virtue. Vices and virtues each work the same way. They start out as a thought, and then become an action and eventually a habit and finally a characteristic. People who develop virtues are known as virtuous, and people who develop vices are vicious.

---

the Fathers of the English Dominican Province

What is key about a virtue is that it is not an automatic characteristic in a person. Just as with any skill or talent, virtues can be deliberately developed through practice. This has huge implications, because faith, hope and love are all considered virtues, but they are treated as accidental qualities which you may or may not have. But if faith is a virtue, this means that we can deliberately foster it…or conversely, we can neglect it and allow it to die in us. Mysteriously, faith, hope and love are also theological virtues, meaning that they are a particular result of God's grace working in us.

I have repeated frequently the maxim that "exterior discipline leads to interior conversion." It is on account of the nature of virtues being something that can be fostered or neglected that this is the case. The luxury budget is an exterior discipline that, if maintained, will lead to a genuine conversion into being a generous person.

But I think when people hear about the luxury budget, they sometimes simply hear "restraint and sacrifice motivated by guilt." Are we martyrs because we moved into a smaller home, because we only have one vehicle (and its old), or because we don't have the latest technology or entertainment available?

The thing is that living this way gives you so much joy and freedom. In the '90s, Lotto 6/49 had the motto, "Imagine the freedom." They meant "imagine the freedom of having millions of dollars and being able to have that house, that car, that vacation, that retirement that were all previously out of reach." But we all know, don't we, that even winning the lottery does not free you from economic concerns, but instead likely loads more of them onto you.

So instead, imagine the freedom of not being a slave of possessions. Imagine the freedom of trusting in God—really trusting in God and not worrying about whether or not He will provide for all of your needs. Imagine the freedom of being able to give generously every time a need arises. These are not just pie-in-the-sky dreams like winning the lottery. This is the freedom that is promised us by the Gospels. No wonder Jesus said, "My yoke is easy, and My burden is light" (Matthew 11:30).

So what virtues are directly opposed to the vice of greed? Obviously, generosity, and I would suggest that practices such as a luxury budget and serving the poor will help us to grow in that area. But there are also other virtues that we can concentrate on that will bring us freedom in this area. For our purposes, we will focus on *gratitude*, *detachment*, and *trusting in God*.

Gratitude

"Rejoice always, pray without ceasing,
give thanks in all circumstances,
for this is the will of God in
Christ Jesus for you."
~1 Thessalonians 5:16–18~

In the biblical narratives, when the Israelites are wandering in the desert after the great Exodus from

Egypt, again and again we see this theme of the people grumbling against God or Moses. It comes to a head in Exodus 17 at Meribah and Massah, where the people are doubting God's providence and asking if God is really with them, despite the fact that He had already provided them with quail and manna and parted the Red Sea. But now they are prepared to stone Moses for having led them into the desert where they were afraid that they would die of thirst.

The story ends with God instructing Moses to strike a rock, from which comes forth water, and so the people can drink, and God proves once again His faithfulness. But it also shows our own human inclination towards grumbling and worrying and how this is an offence against God who is providing for us.

Rather than grumbling, we ought to give thanks.

Back in 2001, I had arranged to meet a friend who wanted to confide in me about some struggle that she was going through. We had arranged to meet on September 11, and of course that was the day that the Twin Towers fell in New York. I kept my appointment anyway and listened attentively as my friend shared her problems, but I remember her saying, "You know, in light of everything that's happening, my problems seem insignificant now."

How often are we guilty of this? You see the phrase on social media all the time: "first world problems." We are complaining about such silly things, and the truth is we have bad days where we're angry because some stranger drove badly and inconvenienced us, or our toilets don't flush properly, or we can't fit all our lawn equipment into our sheds…but rather than grumble we ought to be grateful for what we have. When we recognize that you have more than almost anyone in the world, it really helps us to put our complaints in perspective.

In youth ministry circles, we call this developing an "attitude of gratitude." We chant things like "I want an attitude check," and the kids respond, "I wanna praise the Lord!"

In fact, at my summer camp, we even teach the kids to say, "Praise the Lord!" every time we announce who has been assigned a specific duty.

Imagine if we could foster that attitude about our daily adult lives. This evening my three-year-old daughter stepped in a pile of poop which was inexplicably in my hallway…I can tell you I wasn't yelling praise the Lord about that duty.

This grumbling is just another symptom of our selfish nature, and it needs to be countered with the virtue of gratitude. Remember: exterior discipline leads to interior conversion. If you want to be a more grateful person, a fantastic place to start is something as simple as keeping a gratitude journal. This is a journal that you keep specifically for the purposes of thanking God. Each day you write down three to five things you are grateful for that day; as you keep a running list, it helps you to realize just how much you have to be grateful for. My wife has been doing this for a while and makes a goal of one thousand items for each list; she's already on her fourth list.

Her dedication to that is one of the things I'm grateful for.

Detachment

"The precept of detachment from riches
is obligatory for entrance into the
Kingdom of Heaven."[59]

In 1996–1997, my first year out of high school, I attended the John Paul II Bible School in Radway, Alberta. It was there that I met my wife, and it was there that my faith and character were formed, with a real vision for holiness.

I remember a speaker who spoke one day about detachment. He likened our attachments to worldly things to a cord that tied a bird down and prevented it from flying. "It doesn't matter if the bird is tied down by a string or a rope; it will not be able to fly."

Then he challenged us to consider which things in our lives we needed to be detached from, and to give those things to God. I prayed about it and made a choice to get rid of some music CDs I had that were not affirming to my faith. The CDs were not awful or antithetical to Christianity, but I wanted to take seriously the passage

---

[59] *CCC*, 2544.

which read, "Finally, brothers and sisters, whatever is true, whatever is noble, whatever is right, whatever is pure, whatever is lovely, whatever is admirable—if anything is excellent or praiseworthy—think about such things" (Philippians 4:8). Frankly, my music was causing me to think about things that were not true, noble, right, pure, lovely and admirable, so I felt that clearly, they were a string that was holding me back from God.

Later I threw out a little notebook in which I had been collecting the best apologetic arguments I had found while reading scripture, because I realized that I was reading scripture out of intellectual pride and in order to argue rather than out of a desire to come to know God more fully. (Interestingly, this second sacrifice was much more difficult than the first.)

But this attitude of detachment stuck with me and became fairly defining in my life. In fact, after leaving Bible school, I prided myself on the claim that there was nothing I owned that I wouldn't give away if prompted to do so by God.

I mentioned earlier a time when my bike was stolen. I was nineteen years old, and I didn't have much money at that time and took city transit everywhere I went. I had bought a two-hundred-dollar bike, so it was fairly inexpensive as far as bikes go. But I remember developing this strange kind of attachment to it.

The bike was white and had a neat shimmer to it. One day I was biking through downtown Calgary, and I stopped to talk to a homeless man and give him some money. He admired my bike and told me how he was saving up to get a bike. Well, there was the prompting from God to give him mine…but I didn't. As I left him, I was nagged by the idea that my bike had become more important to me than being generous with God.

It became even more apparent later, when my little brother asked if he could borrow my bike so that he could run to the store.

"No," I said.

"I'll lock it up, and I'm only going to be gone for half an hour."

"No."

"Why not?"

"I just don't want you to."

Now that's a pretty normal conversation for two teenage boys to have, and one that in all likelihood my brother has since forgotten. But I remember it because I remember the wrestling sensation, I had experienced. I occasionally have this sense of interior conflict which impacts my ability to look people in the eye and which even makes my neck behave oddly—kind of like a twitch—and I experienced it that day.

A short time later, it was Holy Thursday, and my church was having all-night adoration. In the middle of the night, I biked to the church and left my bike leaning against the base of the large cross near the adoration chapel.

Inside I began praying that I would put God before everything else in my life, and I prayed to God that if there was anything in my life that I was too attached to, I gave Him permission to take that thing away from me. I suddenly sensed that when I left adoration, my bike would be gone. I knew I had grown too attached to it, and I had just given God permission to take it from me. I resisted the urge to go and check on it. But when I finished my prayers, I left the church, and sure enough, my bike was gone. Feeling a remarkable sense of levity, I walked home praising God.

Now it's not that remarkable that an unlocked bike left leaning against a church in the city in the middle of the night should be stolen. I don't think it was some angelic intervention or anything. But what mattered was the way in which God worked in me through that experience.

Ever since I was a kid, I knew that in today's age, "thou shalt not worship false idols" meant that we should value nothing more than we value God. Anything that is more important than God can become an idol. Christians say that so often, but if I'm honest, I still put several things before God. I still spend my money selfishly, serving Mammon instead of God. I spend my time even more selfishly, dedicating foolish amounts of time to Facebook and other frivolous entertainment sources, while regularly confessing that I did not get enough prayer time in or enough quality time with my family. And I know I have a tendency to put my intelligence and skills and public image and so many other things before God. I suspect that we are all guilty of putting other things before God, at least sometimes.

The question is, from the detachment perspective: what are we willing to give up in order to follow God? Our homes? Our reputations?

In the parable of the Rich Young Man (Matthew 19:16–24), the rich young man asserts that he obeys all of the commandments and has done so since his youth…which, if you ask me, is a remarkable achievement. But Jesus says, "If you want to be perfect, go, sell your possessions and give to the poor, and you will have treasure in Heaven. Then come, follow Me" (Matthew 19:21).

The rich man went away sad, because he had great wealth. This story is actually in all three synoptic Gospels, and each end with Jesus famously saying it is easier for a camel to pass through the eye of a needle than for a rich man to enter Heaven. Why? Because God hates the rich? Of course not. But when we serve wealth, we make it an idol.

Contrast this story with the one about Zacchaeus, the short tax collector who climbed a tree to see Jesus in Luke 19. Jesus comes to his house and eats with him, and Zacchaeus is convicted. He repents, saying, "Behold, Lord, half of my possessions I will give to the poor, and if I have defrauded anyone of anything, I will give back four times as much" (Luke 19:8).

Notice too Jesus' response: "Today salvation has come to this house" (Luke 19:9). So, the rich young man goes away sad and apparently is denied entry into the kingdom because he is too attached to wealth, but salvation comes to Zacchaeus after he spends time with Christ, is moved to repentance, and generously gives his wealth away.

I think the reason that greed is called idolatry, that serving money is incompatible with serving God, and that it is so hard for a rich man to enter Heaven is precisely because our wealth becomes a blockage to the transforming grace of God in our lives. We do not trust in God, but trust instead in our wealth, and Jesus will do nothing where there is no faith (cf. Matthew 13:58).

The challenge of putting God first in our lives is such that everything else should be subservient to Him and His glory. If God asked you to give up your home, or your technology, or your job, could you do it readily, trusting in Him? Is there anything in your life that is holding you back from seeking the kingdom?

"Sell your possessions and give to the poor. Provide purses for yourselves that will not wear out, a treasure in Heaven that will never fail, where no thief comes near, and no moth destroys. For where your treasure is, there your heart will be also" (Luke 12:33–34).

Do Not Worry

"Therefore, I tell you, do not be anxious about your life,
what you will eat or what you will drink,
nor about your body, what you will put on...
which of you by being anxious can add
a single hour to his span of life?"
~Matthew 6:25, 27~

The last virtue I want to discuss is faith. A lot of times
we think of faith as being intellectual assent to a creed
or a set of ideas. But I'm talking about the kind of faith
for which Abraham and the Roman centurion alike
were praised: faith and trust in God that He will do
what He said He would do.

One of the concerns I've often heard about living
simply is that I need to be responsible and prudent and
to care for myself and my children. I have a primary
responsibility to see that my children's needs are met.
This is of course all true, and it is not by accident that
prudence is called the charioteer of the virtues. So of
course, as with all things, moderation is key. However,
I think if we're to be honest, most people err on the side
of selfishness, and very few err on the side of being
overly generous.

The big concern is, of course, what about my
retirement? Look, I'll be honest. I'm putting money
away for that day; I have RRSPs and property. God
willing, I will not starve, and I will not become a
burden to society. However, in this regard, I am living
somewhat inconsistently with my ideals.

Regarding retirement, one scripture passage comes to mind: the Parable of the Rich Fool as found in Luke 12: 13–21. The parable tells of a rich man who had so much abundance that he could not only meet his needs, but he built barns to store grain for later years. And he felt as if he had acted wisely, but God condemned him, saying, "You fool! This very night your life will be demanded from you. Then who will get what you have prepared for yourself?" (Luke 12:21).

I wonder if in my attempts to be wise by worldly standards, am I not in fact doing that which Jesus calls foolish? Perhaps more discernment is necessary. From my research, the Church does not mandate against saving or investing, provided that we invest morally and never forget "the duty of charity…that is, the duty to give from one's 'abundance' and sometimes even out of one's needs, in order to provide what is essential for the life of a poor person."[60]

There is a popular American pastor named Francis Chan, author of *Crazy Love* and several other works, who not only downsized his house and gives 90% of his money away due in part to a similar experience as what I had in Africa, but he does not even save for retirement. When people ask him, "What if things don't work out?" he cites the Parable of the Rich Fool and the passages that follow that one, where Jesus promises that God would take care of our needs. Francis Chan says "Well, I'm taking God at His Word."

---

[60] John Paul II, *Centesimus Annus*, s.36.

I think this leads into another attitude that we need to try to foster in our lives: real, authentic faith that does not worry. Immediately following the Parable of the Rich Fool is Jesus' famous command "Do not worry":

> "Then Jesus said to his disciples: "Therefore I tell you, do not worry about your life, what you will eat; or about your body, what you will wear. For life is more than food, and the body more than clothes. Consider the ravens: they do not sow or reap; they have no storeroom or barn; yet God feeds them. And how much more valuable you are than birds. Who of you by worrying can add a single hour to your life? Since you cannot do this very little thing, why do you worry about the rest? Consider how the wildflowers grow. They do not labour or spin. Yet I tell you, not even Solomon in all his splendour was dressed like one of these. If that is how God clothes the grass of the field, which is here today and tomorrow is thrown into the fire, how much more will He clothe you—you of little faith! And do not set your heart on what you will eat or drink; do not worry about it. For the pagan world runs after all such things, and your Father knows that you need them. But seek his kingdom, and these things will be given to you as well." (Luke 12:22–31)

I don't know about you, but when I hear that passage, it kind of invokes images in my mind of flowers and birds, and I begin to imagine big fluffy clouds flitting by to the sound of hippies playing sitars, and I don't really listen clearly to the message.

But the message is that we should trust in God that He will meet our needs. In fact, when Matthew records the same sermon, he concludes this point with Jesus saying, "Seek first His kingdom and His righteousness, and all these things will be given to you as well" (Matthew 6:33). Taken together, these two accounts of Jesus' Sermon on the Mount tell us that we need not worry and pursue wealth or even security like the pagans do, but rather we need to have faith in God that He will provide for us everything that we need. "Do not worry about tomorrow, for tomorrow will care for itself" (Matthew 6:34).

How many times does Jesus admonish His followers for their lack of faith? Faith is not mere intellectual assent to the truths of God; it is trusting God that He will do as He said. Jesus taught us to call God "Abba," an intimate Aramaic word for *father*, like *daddy* in English.

When Jesus taught us the "Our Father," He taught us to say, "Abba...give us this day our daily bread." It's as if He were borrowing language from Proverbs 30:8–9:

> Give me neither poverty nor riches but give me only my daily bread. Otherwise, I may have too much and disown you and say, "Who is the Lord?"

Our relationship with our Father is not one that asks for wealth, but one that trusts not only in His providence but also in the goodness of His will.

Can I trust my Daddy to take care of me? If God desires that we should meet with hardship, we accept good things from God, so will we not accept bad as well? We need to develop a childlike disposition of trust in our Daddy, who loves us much more than we love ourselves and can provide for us much more abundantly anyway. "Abandonment to the providence of the Father in Heaven frees us from anxiety about tomorrow. Trust in God is a preparation for the blessedness of the poor. They shall see God."[61]

God's Providence

Because of the luxury budget, Catherine and I have very little difficulty living within our means. Frequently we will have a buildup of money in our bank accounts, so that if at that time someone asks us to donate to some ministry, or to help sponsor refugees, or there's an earthquake in Haiti…we have the freedom to give. We're not worried that if we give, we won't have enough for ourselves—because we always have enough for ourselves.

In fact, as mentioned before, when our funds become critically low and it looks as if we may in fact have difficulty making ends meet, my wife will actually give more money away. She works as a day-home provider,

[61] *CCC*, 2547.

which provides a somewhat irregular income. A few months ago, she said, "You know, I haven't had as many kids in the day home this month, so I won't be making as much. We better make an extra donation."

Now what kind of logic is that? It is the logic of faith. Obviously, my wife is a very godly woman. God will not be outdone in generosity.

Scripture is replete with verses that promise things like, "Whoever sows bountifully will reap bountifully" (2 Corinthians 9:6). This is not the prosperity gospel, which some preachers proclaim, asserting that God wants to make us wealthy and will do so if we are generous. But it is a promise that we can trust in Him to take care of us.

This idea that God will make us wealthy—and, usually, healthy as well—is popular in some Christian circles. It does not quite make sense from a Catholic perspective, where there is value even in suffering and in the struggle. Evidence that God's providence does not extend that far can be seen in the lives of the saints, and in the many economic and health hardships they endured while being faithful to God and His plan for their lives. This idea of God making us healthy, and wealthy may be rooted in the concept that the purpose of life is to be happy, which when framed in Christian-speak is, "God intends us to be happy in this life and in the next." This may be true overall, but even more than happy, He wants us to be loving.

I return to the father analogy, since Jesus called God

"Father" and encouraged us to do likewise. I want my kids to be happy, but even more so, I want them to be loving, mature people of character. For this reason, I do not give my five-year-old everything he asks for. Toys, TV programs, freedom and foods: I restrict all of these by my judgment because, while they may make him "happy," I know that this is only for the short-term, and ultimately it would damage his maturity and character and ability to love. In fact, many times I impose upon him things that he did not ask for, even training him to eat carrots and bread crusts. Flossing his teeth is an epic battle every evening.

Sometimes when my son protests, I try to explain it to him, but often he lacks the ability to understand me, and so I just ask him to trust me that what I am willing for him is for his ultimate good. So it is with God; we cannot understand His ways, but even when He disciplines us, this is for our own profit, so that we might partake in His holiness (cf. Hebrews 12:10).

When we remember that love of money is incompatible with Christianity, then it is easy to interpret verses like "Seek first the Kingdom of Heaven and His righteousness, and all these things will be added unto you" (Matthew 6:33). Clearly "all these things" means that God will provide for our needs, but not for all of our wants. God is promising us food, not sports cars.

I always wonder how proponents of the Prosperity Gospel account for the fact that so many Christians in places like Africa are clearly not becoming wealthy despite their fidelity to the Christian message.

The challenge for us is to trust in God and in His providence—not that He will make us wealthy or give us everything that we think we want from a human standpoint, but that He will provide for us the means to fulfill His will in our lives. And of course, His will for our lives is much greater than our own.

Christ doesn't want us to simply change our practices regarding money or to just legalistically tithe while we serve money with the rest of our lives. Christ is interested in transforming our hearts. We are to put to death the old self—the self that was stingy, selfish, covetous and worrisome, slaves to possessions—and we are to be reborn as people who are generous, grateful, detached, and faithful. This transformation can take place in us, through the grace of God, by abiding in him, but we have to cooperate with that grace and be prepared to be completely transformed by Him.

Chapter Seven Discussion Questions

1. "Do not covet." Do you find that when you're shopping you are tempted to buy things that you do not need?

2. Do you enjoy shopping?

3. Do you notice the effect that advertising has on your buying habits?

4. Do you agree that limiting exposure to ads and products would be beneficial to living simply?

5. Is it appropriate to flatter people who buy into materialism and luxury?

6. What are concrete things you can do to practice the virtues that are opposed to greed – gratitude, detachment, faith?

7. Do you struggle to be grateful and recognize the gifts you have, or does it come naturally?

8. Do you keep a gratitude journal? If so, have you noticed an effect on your attitude?

9. We all know that anything we put before God in our lives becomes an idol. What in your life would you have the hardest time giving up if God asked you to? Have you ever had to sacrifice something difficult?

10. Do you worry about finances?

11. Do you believe the maxim "Everything happens for a reason."? Do you at least trust the more scriptural maxim "God works everything to the good of those who love Him."? (Rom 8:28)

12. Do you think saving for retirement is consistent with living simply and trusting in God's providence?

Chapter Eight
For the Sake of the Poor

Okay, so the challenge is to live simply—not for simplicity's sake, but for the sake of love and solidarity with the poor. The whole thing doesn't make sense unless we somehow help the poor. So how do we do that?

This is a complex question, as poverty is caused by a whole host of complicated issues, and sometimes our attempts to solve the problems exacerbate them. Fortunately, in my wisdom, I have determined a sure-fire, foolproof solution to the problem of poverty in all of its forms.

I'm kidding, of course.

I think one of the things that paralyzes us against acting positively against poverty is the complexity of the issues. You hear a lot of good people say, "Just throwing money at the problem won't make it go away." Well, of course not. We should be strategic and deliberate in the efforts that we make. For my part, I don't know what the best or most important solution is. But I know that the complexity of the issue should not prevent us from responding to it in love.

Consider for a moment just how complicated it is. First there are the basic needs. What do you meet first? Clean drinking water? Food? Security? Shelter? Defense against the terrorist groups that threaten some of these people? Education? What happens if we just give food and water and shelter to people; will they then learn to be dependent on foreign handouts and so not take any initiative to grow their own economies?

Maybe to help people be self-sufficient, we should be investing in micro-loans so that the economies of whole regions will grow. What about sweatshops? Is it immoral to buy something cheaply made overseas because the people making it are not being paid a fair wage? On the other hand, should we deliberately buy things that are cheap because it will free up more money to give to the poor? (Provided that we actually will give it, that is.)

Is there an argument to be made that sweatshops are actually the solution to poverty, that people are not forced to work in them but choose to because it is the only employment available to them, and so you are actually investing in their economies by opening a sweatshop in their country?

What about climate change? Pope Francis himself raised this concern within the Church when he wrote *Laudato Si*. Isn't climate change threatening the poor even more than it is the rich? Isn't the refugee crisis caused in part by environmental degradation? Even the war in Syria can be argued to have been caused by a famine resulting from climate change. Maybe we should be investing in clean energy. But is it right to create international standards on carbon emissions when poor countries need the advantage of cheap energy?

What about population control? After all, overpopulation leads to limited resources, famines, and plagues. But are plagues nature's way of thinning a population? Maybe we need diseases for the same reasons that a forest needs fire. Should we be fighting diseases then? Or should we let them run their course?

And on population control, we know that the Catholic Church is at odds with many people trying to champion the rights of the poor. Shouldn't the Church change her teaching on contraception and help distribute condoms to poor people? Shouldn't we make abortion more readily available?

What about the wars? What about the terrorists? What about the geopolitical situation? What about the dictators? What about the corrupt officials who benefit from our attempts at aid? What about the NGOs that use too much of our donated money to pay for promotions and the salaries of their CEOs? Do we help countries with poor human rights records? If everyone started trying to live simply, wouldn't this just undermine the global economy and increase poverty?

It's pretty easy to become overwhelmed by the many factors that need to be considered. So, what's the solution? Honestly...I don't know. I think it would be ridiculous to propose that I do know. But I think to do nothing in light of these issues is a sin, and a grave one. *What* to do? I suggest you do some research and pray and find out what God is calling you to do. It is conceivable that God is calling each of us to give in different ways.

I can share a little light on some of the complications listed above. The Church does address some of these problems in the *Catechism*. First off: sweatshops. Regarding sweatshops, it says;

> "A just wage is the legitimate fruit of work. To refuse or withhold it can be a grave injustice. In determining fair pay both the needs and the contributions of each person must be taken into account. "Remuneration for work should guarantee man the opportunity to provide a dignified livelihood for himself and his family on the material, social, cultural and spiritual level, taking into account the role and the productivity of each, the state of the business, and the common good." Agreement between the parties is not sufficient to justify morally the amount to be received in wages."[62]

The other issue raised above that I want to touch on is the issue of overpopulation. The Catholic Church is often criticized for not cooperating with major charitable and government organizations that want to fight poverty and AIDS by distributing condoms. Pope Francis addresses this conflict it *Laudato Si*:

> "Instead of resolving the problems of the poor and thinking how the world can be different, some can only propose a

---

[62] *CCC*, 2434.

> reduction in the birthrate.... To blame population growth instead of extreme and selective consumerism on the part of some, is one way of refusing to face the issues."[63]

The difficulty with the Catholic Church's teaching on Natural Family Planning is that you kind of have to believe it to get it. It's a "theology of faith seeking understanding" kind of thing, to quote St. Anselm. To do theology, you must believe it before you can understand it. Most people try to understand it before they choose to believe it. They won't believe in the Trinity until they understand the Trinity, but understanding the Trinity is impossible, so we must believe it first and then try to understand it. The Church's teaching on contraception is kind of like that.

 That's not to say that there's no good, rational arguments for the Church's teaching on contraception; there are plenty, and a full exploration of this teaching is clearly well beyond the scope of this book. But to understand it, you first have to assume that human life has profound dignity, which in itself is due to the unique nature of our creation in the image and likeness of God, and as a consequence human sex has profound dignity. It also helps to have a grasp of the concept of natural law.

These things are the basis for all the Church's teachings

---

[63] Francis I, *Laudato Si* (2015 Encyclical Letter), s.50, retrieved from http://www.vatican.va/content/francesco/en/encyclicals/documents/pa pa-francesco_20150524_enciclica-laudato-si.html.

on sexuality, and so her teachings are incomprehensible to anyone who thinks that we simply accidentally evolved or that there is no inherent moral code that sex merely for love and pleasure but not for procreation violates. It seems as though much of the media, and consequently much of our contemporary society, understands merely that the Catholic Church says condoms are sinful. So, these people were bewildered when Pope Benedict XVI said that a male prostitute with HIV would be taking a step in the right direction if he used a condom to prevent the spread of HIV. All many people hear is that the pope is saying condoms may not be wrong in some circumstances…and they think he must therefore be changing Church teaching.

Anyway, the long and the short of it is this: the Church's teaching on contraception is sufficiently sophisticated, that anyone with only a superficial grasp of it is going to miss it, so no wonder they are critical of it. Nonetheless, condoms are not the solution to poverty or to the AIDS problem. As Pope Francis said, people who "blame birthrate instead of extreme and selective consumerism on the part of some (are) refusing to face the issues."[64]

The issues are incredibly complex, and the solution to poverty evades us. However, I do think that if Christians, if even just Catholics who are seriously seeking holiness, would heed the Church and scripture on these matters, we would make a pretty big dent in

---

[64] Francis I, *Laudato Si,* s.50.

poverty. Many of the problems are the result of overconsumption by the rich. If climate change is truly the looming catastrophe that so many scientists tell us it is, and if it is manmade, then it is our patterns of consumption that are driving it. Therefore, by changing the way that we live in this regard, we can simultaneously provide for the needs of the poor today and fight against further environmental degradation in the future.

For those of you who just want a practical answer to the question, "What should I do now?" here's what I suggest:

- Step One: Reduce your consumption and begin living more simply.

- Step Two: Give.

How do you simplify? I suggest the luxury budget of course, but I also suggest that you take a hard look at your lifestyle. Do you really need a second vehicle? Could you make do with secondhand clothes? Are your vacations unnecessarily luxurious? Do you need such a big house? Consider what John Chrysostom thinks of big houses:

> "We build houses that we may have a habitation; not that we may make an ambitious display. What is beyond our wants is superfluous and useless. Put on a sandal that is larger than your foot! You will not endure it, for it is a hindrance to

the step. Thus, also a house larger than necessity requires, is an impediment to your progress towards Heaven. Do you wish to build large and splendid houses? I forbid it not; but let it not be upon the earth! Build thyself tabernacles in Heaven, and such that thou mayest be able to receive others; tabernacles that shall never be dissolved!"[65]

Step Two is the complicated one. This is where you choose what to do with all the money you are saving as a result of Step One. And this is the one where I annoyingly suggest that you do your own research and seek the Lord on what to do.

That's it. Two steps. Consume less; give more. Sparing and sharing.

There have been theological movements that have held that the mission of the Church was, in part, to eradicate poverty and establish the kingdom of God on earth. That's not the mission, by the way; the mission of the Church is to make disciples, but we would be much more effective at that if we worked harder to fight poverty.

Pope Francis said, "Practicing charity is the best way to

---

[65] John Chrysostom, *The Homilies of St. John Chrysostom on the Statues, or, To the People of Antioch*, Homily 2, s.15, retrieved from http://www.documenta-catholica.eu/d_0345-0407-%20Iohannes%20Chrysostomus%20-%20Homilies%20on%20Statues%20-%20EN.pdf.

evangelize."[66]

But supposing, as a thought experiment, that the mission of the Church was to eradicate poverty. How could the Church go about doing it in the face of so many factors?

Is it reasonable to suppose that in such a scenario, God would have each one of us attack poverty from a different angle? What if we were to apply the analogy from St. Paul that we are the body of Christ and are all individual members of it? (cf. Romans 12, 1 Corinthians 12). We are all given our own gifts and hearts for different issues, and all working together we can accomplish our mission.

The mission of the Church may not be to eradicate poverty, but Christians responding in love to the Holy Spirit working in them will of course want to alleviate it where they can. Maybe you have a heart for victims of human trafficking, and you want to pour your resources into that. Maybe it's medicine. Maybe it's education. Imagine again if all Christians, or at least all of us who are striving to live consistent with the Gospel gave abundantly of our time and money and resources to those ministries that we are individually passionate about? Imagine the difference it could make. It almost seems like we could eliminate poverty. Couple with that how much more effective our efforts to evangelize would be: could we see the kingdom of God on earth?

---

[66] Francis I, Twitter post (January 24 2015), retrieved from https://twitter.com/pontifex/status/558918164604399617?lang=en.

I'll put a damper on my own enthusiasm here. Jesus said that the poor will always be with us. So, it seems that eradicating poverty is in fact impossible. We may even miss something in the effort. When we seek to eradicate poverty, are we seeking to make everyone like us, the rich for whom it is so difficult to enter the Kingdom of Heaven? There is beauty and value in poverty and dependence. Perhaps the goal of eliminating poverty itself is born of our materialistic value system. Perhaps we should eliminate destitution and seek to love poverty?

I think of St. Francis of Assisi who sought "Lady Poverty" as though she were a beautiful woman that he wanted to court. I wonder what he would say about our ambitions to eradicate poverty. But here we are again, with the saints challenging us to go further than I am willing to go.

This calls for wisdom. There is an orphanage that I visit in Mexico City when I go there on missions. It was founded by a lady who has been called the "Mother Teresa of Mexico." Mother Inez started the orphanage fifty years ago when she had compassion on two homeless orphans. She chose to leave her convent and become homeless herself to care for them. Today she cares for two hundred and thirty orphans in her home.

Many of the children are not really orphans but have been abandoned because of severe handicaps. When we visit, our mission is just to show love to them—play with them, sing to them, touch them—because the staff at the orphanage cannot do those things as much as the kids need.

It struck me that all of us cry when we see the children. But Mother Inez does not cry; she smiles. I suspect that if we change our goal from eradication of poverty and suffering to love of those who are poor and suffering, we will discover what she knows.

I will tell you about the organization I choose to (primarily) give to. For whatever reason, my heart goes to the organizations that sponsor children. The idea that I can give a child an education, food, clothing, and medicine—that I can meet that one child's essential needs for just over one dollar each day—strikes me as being the best use of my money. This also becomes a very handy framework for determining whether the purchase I want to make is justified or not. If I want to make an unnecessary forty-dollar purchase, I need only to consider that by not purchasing it, I can sponsor a child for an entire month.

Of the organizations that sponsor children, I choose Chalice, (Chalice.ca) because it is a Canadian Catholic organization that gives 91.3% of its revenues directly into their programs overseas. I compared this with two other major sponsorship organizations, and they directed 85.7% and 80.9% to their programming. *Money Sense Magazine* grades charities on their efficiency and governance, and for the last five years in a row, Chalice was given an A+ grade, making it among the best charities being examined by *Money Sense Magazine*.[67]

I don't give all my money to just one charity; I have a number of favourites. Again, one of the beauties of living simply so you can live generously is that whenever an issue arises, you have the money to give where it needs to be given.

Do not be overwhelmed by the complexity of helping people. I suggest you simply take to heart the command of Jesus: "Do to others as you would have them do to you" (Luke 6:31). Whatever issue you are passionate about, respond generously, and trust that God will bring your gift to fruition.

The call to live simply is a call for everyone. We rich Christians must respond generously and faithfully to the Word of God, as contained both in scripture and in the teachings of the Catholic Church. Though the issues are complicated, the call to repentance is straightforward:

Spend less; give more.

I pray that each one of us will have the courage and discernment to seek God's voice and to do His will.

---

[67] Mark Brown, "2017 Charity 100: Grades," *Money Sense Magazine* (November 16, 2016), retrieved from http://www.moneysense.ca/planning/2016-charity-100-grades/.

Chapter Eight Discussion Questions

1. When you want to be generous, do you feel overwhelmed by all the competing factors that you need to consider in who to give to?

2. What is your favorite charity, and why?

3. What cause do you care about the most?

4. Should we be more concerned with local causes, or should causes on distant continents be just as important?

5. Some justice issues, like climate change and sweatshops and deforestation, are driven by consumption. But it seems that even those advocating for change in these areas advocate for political and taxation policies, rather than for behavioral change in individuals. Discuss how the reduction of our personal consumption may actually affect these issues.

6. St. John Chrysostom makes an analogy between sandals sizes and house sizes, saying that in both cases if it's too big they will hinder progress. (Pg 156) Do you think people in the west live in houses that are sized correctly for their family needs? Do you know of anyone who has deliberately downsized in order to be more generous with their wealth?

Do you find that a too big house is a hindrance to growth?

7. Imagine if all faith filled Catholics heeded the call to live simply and generously. How would that affect our mission of evangelization? What impact would that have on global poverty? Is eradicating global poverty possible?

Appendix

Scripture Passages Regarding Simplicity

"Your prayers and your gifts to the poor have come up as a memorial offering before God." ~ Acts 10:4

"But now I am writing to you that you must not associate with anyone who claims to be a brother or sister but is sexually immoral or greedy, an idolater or slanderer, a drunkard or swindler. Do not even eat with such people." ~ 1 Corinthians 5:11 (cf. 1 Corinthians 6:9–10, Ephesians 5:5, and Colossians 3:5)

"They gave as much as they were able, and even beyond their ability." ~ 2 Corinthians 8:3

"Our desire is not that others might be relieved while you are hard pressed, but that there might be equality. At the present time your plenty will supply what they need, so that in turn their plenty will supply what you need. The goal is equality, as it is written: 'The one who gathered much did not have too much, and the one who gathered little did not have too little.'" ~ 2 Corinthians 8:13–15

"So I thought it necessary to encourage the brothers to go on ahead to you and arrange in advance for your promised gift, so that in this way it might be ready as a bountiful gift and not as an exaction. Consider this: whoever sows sparingly will also reap sparingly, and whoever sows bountifully will also reap bountifully.

Each must do as already determined, without sadness or compulsion, for God loves a cheerful giver. Moreover, God is able to make every grace abundant for you, so that in all things, always having all you need, you may have an abundance for every good work." ~ 2 Corinthians 9:5–8

"Whoever loves money never has enough; Whoever loves wealth is never satisfied with their income. This too is meaningless. As goods increase, so do those who consume them. And what benefit are they to the owners except to feast their eyes on them? The sleep of a labourer is sweet, whether they eat little or much, But as for the rich, their abundance permits them no sleep." ~ Ecclesiastes 5:10–12

"I will search for the lost and bring back the strays. I will bind up the injured and strengthen the weak, but the sleek and the strong I will destroy. I will shepherd the flock with justice. As for you, my flock, this is what the Sovereign Lord says: 'I will judge between one sheep and another, and between rams and goats. Is it not enough for you to feed on the good pasture? Must you also trample the rest of your pasture with your feet? Is it not enough for you to drink clear water? Must you also muddy the rest with your feet? Must My flock feed on what you have trampled and drink what you have muddied with your feet?' Therefore this is what the Sovereign Lord says to them: 'See, I Myself will judge between the fat sheep and the lean sheep. Because you shove with flank and shoulder, butting all the weak sheep with your horns until you have driven them away,

I will save My flock, and they will no longer be plundered. I will judge between one sheep and another.'" ~ Ezekiel 34:16–22

"Keep your lives free from the love of money and be content with what you have, because God has said, 'Never will I leave you; never will I forsake you.'" ~ Hebrews 13:5

"Religion that God our Father accepts as pure and faultless is this: to look after orphans and widows in their distress and to keep oneself from being polluted by the world." ~ James 1:27

"Suppose a brother or a sister is without clothes and daily food. One of you says to them, "Go in peace; keep warm and well fed" but does nothing about their physical needs; what good is it? In the same way, faith by itself, if it is not accompanied by action, is dead." ~ James 2:15–17

"Now listen, you rich people, weep and wail because of the misery that is coming on you. Your wealth has rotted, and moths have eaten your clothes. Your gold and silver are corroded. Their corrosion will testify against you and eat your flesh like fire. You have hoarded wealth in the last days. Look! The wages you failed to pay the workers who mowed your fields are crying out against you. The cries of the harvesters have reached the ears of the Lord Almighty. You have lived on earth in luxury and self-indulgence. You have fattened yourselves in the day of slaughter." ~ James 5: 1–5

"Give to everyone who asks you." ~ Luke 6:30

"If anyone has material possessions and sees a brother or sister in need but has no pity on them, how can the love of God be in that person? Dear children, let us not love with words or speech but with actions and in truth." ~ 1 John 3:17–18

 "Whoever claims to love God yet hates a brother or sister is a liar. For whoever does not love their brother and sister, whom they have seen, cannot love God, whom they have not seen." ~ 1 John 4:20

"He has filled the hungry with good things, but the rich He has sent away empty." ~ Luke 1:53

"Anyone who has two shirts should share with the one who has none, and anyone who has food should do the same." ~ Luke 3:11

"Blessed are you who are poor, for yours is the kingdom of God" ~ Luke 6:20

"Woe to you who are rich; you have received your comfort." ~ Luke 6:24

"Be generous to the poor, and everything will be clean for you." ~ Luke 11:41

The Parable of the Rich Fool, who puts all his grain in barns saving up for the future, and then dies and loses it all, with God saying, "You fool!" Jesus sums it up by saying, "This is how it will be for whoever stores up things for themselves but is not rich towards God." ~ Luke 12:16–21

"Sell your possessions and give to the poor. Provide purses for yourself that will never wear out, a treasure in Heaven that will never fail, where no thief comes near and no moth destroys." ~ Luke 12:33

Lazarus and the Rich Man ~ Luke 16:19–31

"'Will a mere mortal rob God? Yet you rob me.'
'But you ask, 'How are we robbing you?'
'In tithes and offerings. You are under a curse—your whole nation—because you are robbing me. Bring the whole tithe into the storehouse, that there may be food in my house. Test me in this,' says the Lord Almighty, 'and see if I will not throw open the floodgates of heaven and pour out so much blessing that there will not be room enough to store it.'" ~ Malachi 3:8–10

"They all gave out of their wealth; but she, out of her poverty, put in everything—all she had to live on." ~ Mark 12:41–44

"In the same way, let your light shine before others, that they may see your good deeds and glorify your Father in Heaven." ~ Matthew 5:16

"No one can serve two masters. Either you will hate the one and love the other, or you will be devoted to the one and despise the other. You cannot serve both God and money." ~ Matthew 6:24

"The seed falling among the thorns refers to someone who hears the Word, but the worries of this life and the deceitfulness of wealth choke the Word, making it unfruitful." ~ Matthew 13:22

"If you want to be perfect, go sell your possessions and give to the poor." ~ Matthew 19:21

"It is harder for a rich man to enter the Kingdom of Heaven than for a camel to pass through the eye of a needle." ~ Matthew 19:24 (cf. Mark 10:25, Luke 18:25)

Jesus' description of the separation of the sheep from the goats when He comes again, with sheep invited into their inheritance with him and goats cast into the eternal fire, based on the questions, "When I was hungry, did you feed me? When I was thirsty, did you give me drink?" etc. ~ Matthew 25:31–46

"Whoever is generous to the poor lends to the Lord, and He will repay him for his deed." ~ Proverbs 19:17

"Give me neither poverty nor riches; feed me with the food that is needful for me, lest I be full and deny you and say, 'Who is the Lord?'" ~ Proverbs 30:8–9

"How joyful are those who fear the Lord…they share freely and give generously to those in need." ~ Psalm 112:1, 9

 "Dress modestly…not with…gold or pearls or expensive clothes." ~ 1 Timothy 2:9–10

"For we have brought nothing into the world, so we cannot take anything out of it either. If we have food and covering, with these we shall be content. But those who want to get rich fall into temptation and a snare and many foolish and harmful desires which plunge men into ruin and destruction. For the love of money is a root of all sorts of evil, and some by longing for it have wandered away from the faith and pierced themselves with many griefs. But flee from these things, you man of God, and pursue righteousness, godliness, faith, love, perseverance and gentleness." ~ 1 Timothy 6:7–11

"The love of money is the root of every evil." ~ 1 Timothy 6:10

"But mark this: There will be terrible times in the last days. People will be lovers of themselves, lovers of money, boastful, proud, abusive, disobedient to their parents, ungrateful, unholy…" ~ 2 Timothy 3:1–2

"Set aside part of your goods for almsgiving. Never turn your face from the poor, and God will never turn His from you. Measure your alms by what you have; if you have much, give more; if you have little, do not be afraid to give less in alms. So doing, you will lay up for yourself a great treasure for the day of necessity. For almsgiving delivers from death and saves people from passing down to darkness. Almsgiving is a most effective offering for all those who do it in the presence of the Most High." ~ Tobit 4:7–11

Catholic Church Teachings

"Hence it must needs be that man's good in their respect consists in a certain measure, in other words, that man seeks, according to a certain measure, to have external riches, in so far as they are necessary for him to live in keeping with his condition of life. Wherefore it will be a sin for him to exceed this measure, by wishing to acquire or keep them immoderately. This is what is meant by covetousness, which is defined as 'immoderate love of possessing.' It is therefore evident that covetousness is a sin." Thomas Aquinas, *Summa Theologiae,* II-II, Q. 118, Art. 1

"Covetousness may signify immoderation about external things in two ways. First, so as to regard immediately the acquisition and keeping of such things, when, to wit, a man acquires or keeps them more than is due. On this way it is a sin directly against one's neighbour, since one man cannot over-abound in external riches, without another man lacking them..." ~ Thomas Aquinas, *Summa Theologiae*, II-II, Q. 118, Art. 1. ad 2

"The bread which you hold back belongs to the hungry; the coat, which you guard in your locked storage-chests, belongs to the naked." ~ St. Basil the Great, "Homily on the saying of the *Gospel According to Luke,* 'I will pull down my barns and build bigger ones,' and on greed," s.7

"By a certain wily artifice of the devil, countless pretexts of expenditure are proposed to the rich." ~ St. Basil the Great, *Sermon to the Rich*, s.2

"Our Lord warns us that we shall be separated from Him if we fail to meet the serious needs of the poor and the little ones who are His brethren." ~ *Catechism of the Catholic Church (CCC),* 1033

"In economic matters, respect for the human dignity requires the practice of the virtue of temperance, so as to moderate attachment to this world's goods, the practice of the virtue of justice, to preserve our neighbour's rights and render him what is his due; and the practice of solidarity, in accordance with the Golden Rule." ~ *CCC,* 2407

"The disordered desire for money cannot but produce perverse effects." ~ *CCC,* 2424

"Love for the poor is even one of the motives for the duty of working so as to be able to give to those in need." ~ *CCC,* 2444

"Love for the poor is incompatible with immoderate love of riches or their selfish use.

'Come now, you rich, weep and howl for the miseries that are coming upon you. Your riches have rotted and your garments are moth-eaten. Your gold and silver have rusted, and their rust will be evidence against you and will eat your flesh like fire. You have laid up treasure for the last days. Behold, the wages of the labourers who mowed your fields, which you kept back by fraud, cry out; and the cries of the harvesters have reached the ears of the Lord of Hosts. You have lived on the earth in luxury and in pleasure; you have fattened your hearts in a day of slaughter. You have condemned, you have killed the righteous man; he does not resist you.'" ~ *CCC,* 2445

"St. John Chrysostom vigorously recalls this: 'Not to enable the poor to share in our goods is to steal from them and deprive them of life. The goods we possess are not ours, but theirs.' 'The demands of justice must be satisfied first of all; that which is already due in justice is not to be offered as a gift of charity.'

"When we attend to the needs of those in want, we give them what is theirs, not ours. More than performing works of mercy, we are paying a debt of justice." ~ *CCC,* 2446

"Detachment from riches is obligatory for entrance into the Kingdom of Heaven." ~ *CCC* 2544

"Abandonment to the providence of the Father in Heaven frees us from anxiety about tomorrow. Trust in God is a preparation for the blessedness of the poor. They shall see God." ~ *CCC,* 2547

"We build houses that we may have a habitation; not that we may make an ambitious display. What is beyond our wants is superfluous and useless. Put on a sandal that is larger than your foot! You will not endure it, for it is a hindrance to the step. Thus also a house larger than necessity requires, is an impediment to your progress towards Heaven. Do you wish to build large and splendid houses? I forbid it not; but let it not be upon the earth! Build thyself tabernacles in Heaven, and such that thou mayest be able to receive others; tabernacles that shall never be dissolved! Why art that mad about fleeting things; and things that must be left here? Nothing is more fallacious than wealth. Today it is for thee; tomorrow it is against thee. It arms the eyes of the envious everywhere. It is a hostile comrade, a domestic enemy; and ye are witnesses of this, who possess it, and are in every way burying it and concealing it from view; as even now too our very wealth makes the danger more insupportable to us."

~ John Chrysostom, *The Homilies of St. John Chrysostom on the Statues, or, To the People of Antioch*, Homily 2, s.15

"Those who bestow laudatory addresses on the rich appear to me to be rightly judged not only flatterers and base, in vehemently pretending that things which are disagreeable give them pleasure, but also godless and treacherous; godless, because neglecting to praise and glorify God, who is alone perfect and good, of whom are all things, and by whom are all things, and for whom are all things, (Romans 11:36) they invest with divine honours men wallowing in an execrable and abominable life, and, what is the principal thing, liable on this account to the judgment of God; and treacherous, because, although wealth is of itself sufficient to puff up and corrupt the souls of its possessors, and to turn them from the path by which salvation is to be attained, they stupefy them still more, by inflating the minds of the rich with the pleasures of extravagant praises, and by making them utterly despise all things except wealth, on account of which they are admired; bringing, as the saying is, fire to fire, pouring pride on pride, and adding conceit to wealth, a heavier burden to that which by nature is a weight, from which somewhat ought rather to be removed and taken away as being a dangerous and deadly disease." ~ Clement of Alexandria, "Who Is the Rich Man That Shall Be Saved?", s.1

"God gave the earth to the whole human race for the sustenance of all its members, without excluding or favouring anyone." ~ *Compendium of the Social Doctrine of the Church* (2004), 171

"Goods, even when legitimately owned, always have a universal destination; any type of improper accumulation is immoral, because it openly contradicts the universal destination assigned to all goods by the Creator." *Compendium of the Social Doctrine of the Church,* 328

"The rich man—St. Gregory the Great will later say—is only an administrator of what he possesses; giving what is required to the needy is a task that is to be performed with humility because the goods do not belong to the one who distributes them. He who retains riches for himself is not innocent; giving to those in need means paying a debt." ~ *Compendium of the Social Doctrine of the Church,* 329

"If you have two coats, you've stolen one from the poor." ~ attributed to servant of God Dorothy Day

"If we are close to Christ and are following in his footsteps, we will wholeheartedly love poverty, privation and detachment from earthly things." ~ St. Josemaría Escrivá, *The Forge* (2003), 997

"Today, the scientific community realizes what the poor have long told us: harm, perhaps irreversible harm, is being done to the ecosystem. The earth, entire peoples and individual persons are being brutally punished. And behind all this pain, death and destruction there is the stench of what Basil of Caesarea called "the dung of the devil". An unfettered pursuit of money rules. The service of the common good is left behind. Once capital becomes an idol and guides people's decisions, once greed for money presides over the entire socioeconomic system, it ruins society, it condemns and enslaves men and women, it destroys human fraternity, it sets people against one another and, as we clearly see, it even puts at risk our common home." ~ Francis I, Address at the Second World Meeting for Popular Movements, Bolivia (July 9, 2015), s.1

"A way has to be found to enable everyone to benefit from the fruits of the earth, and not simply to close the gap between the affluent and those who must be satisfied with the crumbs falling from the table, but above all to satisfy the demands of justice, fairness and respect for every human being." ~ Francis I, Address to the 38th Conference of the Food and Agricultural Organization of the United Nations (June 20, 2013), s.1

"The times talk to us of so much poverty in the world and this is a scandal. Poverty in the world is a scandal. In a world where there is so much wealth, so many resources to feed everyone, it is unfathomable that there are so many hungry children, that there are so many children without an education, so many poor persons. Poverty today is a cry." ~ Francis I, "Address to the Students of the Jesuit Schools of Italy and Albania" (June 7, 2013)

"Money must serve, not rule! The Pope loves everyone, rich and poor alike, but he is obliged in the name of Christ to remind all that the rich must help, respect and promote the poor. I exhort you to generous solidarity and a return of economics and finance to an ethical approach which favours human beings." Francis I, *Evangelii Gaudium* (2013 Apostolic Exhortation), s.38

"Almost without being aware of it, we end up being incapable of feeling compassion at the outcry of the poor, weeping for other people's pain, and feeling a need to help them, as though all this were someone else's responsibility and not our own. The culture of prosperity deadens us; we are thrilled if the market offers us something new to purchase; and in the meantime all those lives stunted for lack of opportunity seem a mere spectacle; they fail to move us." ~ Francis I, *Evangelii Gaudium* (2013 Apostolic Exhortation), s.54

"Consumerism has accustomed us to waste. But throwing food away is like stealing it from the poor and hungry." ~ Francis I, Twitter post (June 7, 2013)

"Practicing charity is the best way to evangelize." ~ Francis I, Twitter post (January 24, 2015)

"A Christian who is too attached to riches has lost his way." ~ Francis I, Twitter post (August 25, 2015)

"The Church's love for the poor is a part of her constant tradition." ~ John Paul II, *Centesimus Annus* (1991 Encyclical Letter), s.57

The Universal Destination of Goods is "the first principle of the whole ethical and social order" and "the characteristic principle of Catholic social doctrine." ~ John Paul II, *Laborem Exercens* (1981 Encyclical), s.19; and *Sollicitudo Rei Socialis* (1987 Encyclical Letter), s.42

"A disconcerting conclusion about the most recent period should serve to enlighten us: side-by-side with the miseries of underdevelopment, themselves unacceptable, we find ourselves up against a form of super-development, equally inadmissible, because like the former it is contrary to what is good and to true happiness. This super-development, which consists in an excessive availability of every kind of material goods for the benefit of certain social groups, easily makes people slaves of 'possession' and of immediate gratification, with no other horizon than the multiplication or continual replacement of the things already owned with others still better. This is the so-called civilization of 'consumption' or 'consumerism,' which involves so much 'throwing-away' and 'waste.' An object already owned but now superseded by something better is discarded, with no thought of its possible lasting value in itself, nor of some other human being who is poorer." ~ John Paul II, *Sollicitudo Rei Socialis* (1987 Encyclical Letter), s.28

"The right to private property is not absolute and unconditional. No one may appropriate surplus goods solely for his own private use when others lack the necessities of life." Paul VI, *Populorum Progressio* (1967 Encyclical), s.23

References

Alcorn, Randy. *Money, Possessions and Eternity*. Carol Stream, IL: Tyndale House Publishers, 2003.

Aquinas, Thomas. *Summa Theologiae*. Translated by the Fathers of the English Dominican Province. Washington, DC; Coyote Canyon Press; 2018

St. Augustine. *On the Sermon on the Mount,* Book 1. Translated by William Findlay. Edited by Philip Schaff. In *Nicene and Post-Nicene Fathers*, First Series, Vol. 6. Buffalo, NY: Christian Literature Publishing Co., 1888.

St. Basil the Great. "Homily on the saying of the *Gospel According to Luke,* 'I will pull down my barns and build bigger ones,' and on greed."

Retrieved from https://bekkos.wordpress.com/2009/10/08/st-basil-on-stealing-from-the-poor/.

St. Basil the Great. "Sermon to the Rich." Retrieved from http://stjohngoc.org/st-basil-the-greats-sermon-to-the-rich/.

Bethune, Brian. "Pope Francis: How the first New World pontiff could save the church." *Maclean's* (March 26, 2013). Retrieved from https://www.macleans.ca/news/world/man-of-the-people-2/.

Brown, Mark. "2017 Charity 100: Grades." *Money Sense Magazine* (November 16, 2016). Retrieved from http://www.moneysense.ca/planning/2016-charity-100-

grades/.

Catechism of the Catholic Church. New York: Doubleday, 1994.

Chrysostom, John. *The Homilies of St. John Chrysostom on the Statues, or, To the People of Antioch,* Homily 2, s.15. Retrieved from http://www.documenta-catholica.eu/d_0345-0407-%20Iohannes%20Chrysostomus%20-%20Homilies%20on%20Statues%20-%20EN.pdf.

Clement of Alexandria. "Who Is the Rich Man That Shall Be Saved?" In The *Ante-Nicene Fathers: The Writings of the Early Church Fathers Down to A.D. 325,* Vol. 2. Translated by Phillip Schaff et. al. Edinburgh: T&T Publishers, 1885.

Canadian Conference of Catholic Biships (CCCB). *Compendium of the Social Doctrine of the Church.* Ottawa: CCCB Publications, 2005.

de Balaguer, Escrivá. *Conversations with Monsignor Escrivá de Balaguer,* 2nd ed. Dublin: Ecclesia Press, 1972.

Dubay, Thomas, S.M. *Happy Are You Poor: The Simple Life and Spiritual Freedom.* San Francisco: Ignatius Press, 1981.

Dubay, Thomas, S.M. *Happy Are You Poor: The Simple Life and Spiritual Freedom.* San Francisco: Ignatius Press, 2003.

Escrívá, St. Josemaría. *The Forge*. 1987. Retrieved from http://www.escrivaworks.org/book/the_forge.htm

Escrívá, St. Josemaría. *Friends of God*. 1977. Retrieved from http://www.escrivaworks.org/book/friends_of_god.htm.

Escrívá, St. Josemaría. *The Way*. 1939. Retrieved from http://www.escrivaworks.org/book/the_way.htm.

Francis I. "Address at the Second World Meeting of Popular Movements" (Bolivia), July 9, 2015. Retrieved from http://www.vatican.va/content/francesco/en/speeches/2015/july/documents/papa-francesco_20150709_bolivia-movimenti-popolari.html.

Francis I. "Address to Participants in the 38th Conference of the Food and Agricultural Organization of the United Nations (FAO)." June 20, 2013. Retrieved from http://www.vatican.va/content/francesco/en/speeches/2013/june/documents/papa-francesco_20130620_38-sessione-fao.html.

Francis I. "Address to the Students of the Jesuit Schools of Italy and Albania," June 7, 2013. Retrieved from http://www.vatican.va/content/francesco/en/speeches/2013/june/documents/papa-francesco_20130607_scuole-gesuiti.html.

Francis I. "Angelus," September 22, 2019. Retrieved from http://www.vatican.va/content/francesco/en/angelus/2019/documents/papa-francesco_angelus_20190922.html.

Francis I. *Evangelii Gaudium*. 2013 Encyclical Letter. Retrieved from http://www.vatican.va/content/francesco/en/apost_exhortations/documents/papa-francesco_esortazione-ap_20131124_evangelii-gaudium.html

Francis I. *Laudato Si.* 2015 Apostolic Exhortation. Retrieved from http://www.vatican.va/content/francesco/en/encyclicals/documents/papa-francesco_20150524_enciclica-laudato-si.html.

Francis I. Twitter account: https://twitter.com/pontifex/.

St. Francis of Assisi. *First Rule* (1221). Retrieved from https://www.sacred-texts.com/chr/wosf/.

Gray, Timothy. *Encountering the Poor: Biblical Roots for Catholic Social Teaching* [CD]. Greenwood Village, CO: Lighthouse Catholic Media, 2014.

John of the Cross. *Ascent of Mount Carmel*. Peabody, Ma; Dover Publications; December 9, 2008

John Paul II. *Centesimus Annus*. 1991 Encyclical Letter. [*Centesimus Annus* is an encyclical letter addressed by the Supreme Pontiff John Paul II to his venerable brothers in the episcopate, the priests and deacons, families of men and women religious, all the

Christian faithful and to all men and women of good will on the hundredth anniversary of *Rerum Novarum*.] Retrieved from http://www.vatican.va/content/john-paul-ii/en/encyclicals/documents/hf_jp-ii_enc_01051991_centesimus-annus.html.

John Paul II. *Laborem Exercens*. 1981 Encyclical. Retrieved from http://www.vatican.va/content/john-paul-ii/en/encyclicals/documents/hf_jp-ii_enc_14091981_laborem-exercens.html.

John Paul II. "Message for the 2004 World Day of Peace," January 1, 2004. Retrieved from http://www.vatican.va/content/john-paul-ii/en/messages/peace/documents/hf_jp-ii_mes_20031216_xxxvii-world-day-for-peace.html.

John Paul II. *Sollicitudo Rei Socialis*. 1987 Encyclical Letter. Retrieved from http://www.vatican.va/content/john-paul-ii/en/encyclicals/documents/hf_jp-ii_enc_30121987_sollicitudo-rei-socialis.html.

Paul VI. *Populorum Progressio*. 1967 Encyclical. Retrieved from http://w2.vatican.va/content/paul-vi/en/encyclicals/documents/hf_p-vi_enc_26031967_populorum.html.

Sider, Ronald J. *Rich Christians in an Age of Hunger: Moving from Affluence to Generosity*. Nashville: Thomas Nelson, 2010.

Slater, Thomas. "Justice." In *The Catholic Encyclopedia,* Vol. 8. New York: Robert Appleton

Company, 1910. Retrieved November 15, 2015 from http://www.newadvent.org/cathen/08571c.htm.

Tuberville, Henry, D.D. *The Douay Catechism of 1649.* New York: P.J. Kennedy, Excelsior Catholic Publishing Hous

About The Author

Peter van Kampen is a writer, a youth pastor, a former program coordinator for Our Lady Of Victory Summer Camp, a father and a husband. He lives in Rocky Mountain House, Alberta and has organized and participated in many mission trips. Peter's enthusiasm for Jesus is contagious, as is the example he sets in how he lives his life, both of which are gifts for the students he works with and the readers who read his books.

Other Books by Peter van Kampen
The Fullness of Time
The Battle for Moriah

9 7 8 1 0 6 9 0 4 1 4 2 5